# A Self-Study Course in Wei Stone Inscriptions

Compiled and written by Huang Quanxin

**SINOLINGUA**

**BEIJING**

First Edition    1998

ISBN 7-80052-457-4

Copyright 1998 by Sinolingua

Published by Sinolingua

24 Baiwanzhuang Road, Beijing 100037, China

Printed by Chunlei Printing House

Distributed by China International

Book Trading Corporation

35 Chegongzhuang Xilu, P.O. Box 399

Beijing 100044, China

*Printed in the People's Republic of China*

# Foreword

Chinese calligraphy, the core of the Oriental arts, reflects the temperament of the Chinese nation. The black and white, dots and lines are an expression of the spirits and images of Nature, reflecting a calligrapher's feelings and knowledge. Calligraphy's profound artistic essence lies in the combination of feeling and rationale, form and spirit, rich structure and vivid rhythm – a perfect balance between the form and the ideological content expressed in a character. Though devoid of color, calligraphy is variously colored as painting; and without sound, it contains melodies just like music.

Chinese calligraphy has a long history, ranging from the keeping of records by tying knots before Cang Jie invented writing, to the characters on earthenware discovered at Dawenkou and inscriptions on bones or tortoise shells of the Shang Dynasty (c. 16th-11th century BC). Like a long running river, Chinese calligraphy has evolved during thousands of years, characterized by simplicity and unsophistication in the Shang and Zhou dynasties (c. 16th century-221 BC), splendor in the Qin and Han dynasties (221 BC-AD 220), graceful bearing in the Wei and Jin dynasties (220-420), magnificence in the Sui and Tang dynasties (581-907), radiating vigor in the Song and Yuan dynasties (960-1368), prosperity in the Ming and Qing dynasties (1368-1911) and grandeur in the current era.

Chinese characters fall into the following styles: regular, running, grass, official and seal scripts. Seal scripts may be divided into large and small characters; official scripts, into Qin and Han styles; grass characters, into *Zhang* (cursive official), *Jin* (modern) and *Kuang* (wild) scripts; and regular characters, into Wei and Tang scripts. Chinese calligraphy not only reflects the character of individual calligrapher, but also presents the styles and flavors of different regions and eras.

China has always regarded calligraphy as the quintessence of Chinese culture and a national treasure as well. Calligraphy is a required course at school and every educated person must study calligraphy.

The art of Chinese calligraphy is unprecedentedly prosperous now. Various kinds of calligraphy model books have been published; however, it is hard to find one which can scientifically instruct people in learning calligraphy. An old saying goes: ``If one owns the best book, one may obtain medium-level knowledge; and if one has a medium-level book, one may only absorb low-level knowledge." Anyone who wishes to have a good command of Chinese calligraphy must have a good teacher and a good book. At the present time when it is hard to find a good teacher, good teaching materials are even more important.

To meet the demands of the people who are interested in Chinese calligraphy, Professor Huang Quanxin has compiled the *Chinese Calligraphy Teach-Yourself Series* in six books: *A Self-Study Course in Regular Script, A Self-Study Course in Wei Stone Inscriptions, A Self-Study Course in Running Script, A Self-Study Course in Grass Script, A Self-Study Course in Official Script,* and *A Self-Study Course in Seal Script*. Each book consists of the following chapters: A Brief Introduction, Techniques, Strokes, Radicals, Structure, The Art of Composition, Creation, Copying, and Appreciation, which should help beginners learn the rudiments, and other learners improve their calligraphy techniques.

With standard model characters, systematic theories for self-study, illustration and texts, the *Chinese Calligraphy Teach-Yourself Series* is well formatted, informative and interesting. Student may appreciate Chinese calligraphy while practicing the models in the books to improve their accomplishments and techniques. We sincerely wish they are of help with the study of Chinese calligraphy.

**Editor**
**October 1994**

# About the Author

Huang Quanxin is a senior teacher of fine arts in the Middle School Attached to Beijing Normal University and a member of the Chinese Calligraphers' Association. In his childhood, he took up the study of calligraphy and paintings, and read a large number of poems. His father was a student of Kang Youwei (a famous reformist in the late Qing Dynasty). For many years, he has lived in Liulichang (an ancient cultural street in Beijing), taken many famous calligraphers, scholars and experts as his teachers, and immersed himself untiringly among calligraphy and painting. When he was a middle-school student, he won first place in a calligraphy contest. Later many more works won awards at important calligraphy competitions and have been exhibited at home and abroad. In addition, he has inscribed the titles of many newspapers and magazines. He is named as an eminent person of the contemporary era by the Calligraphy Association of Wang Xizhi's hometown, included in the book *Famous Calligraphers in Beijing* by the Beijing Calligraphers' Association, as well as in *A Dictionary of Chinese Artists of the Present Age* and *Who's Who in the World*.

Huang Quanxin is also a member of the Chinese Society for Fine Arts Education and a standing council member of the district society. In his youth, he compiled teaching materials for the fine arts, painted color picture-story books, and created hanging paintings, which were named by the State Education Commission as excellent works. He visited Taiwan as a member of the artists delegation from mainland China and held a one-man calligraphy show in Japan. Many of his calligraphy works and paintings have been sent by the government officials to foreign guests as gifts, enjoying a high reputation both at home and abroad. Hence he is included in the book *Famous Chinese Painters*.

Huang Quanxin has served as teacher for thirty years, with students from all over the country and some in foreign countries. Quite a number of his students came out top at many domestic and international calligraphy and paintings competitions.

Huang Quanxin founded the first parents' school in Beijing and has served as head of the National Excellent Parents' School for many years. He is a consultant of Beijing primary and middle-school education, a former host of an education program of Beijing Broadcasting Station, one of the compilers of the teaching materials and courses of the Beijing Parents' School, a member of the Beijing Research Association of Family Education and a council member of the district research association. He is also interested in various aspects of Chinese traditional culture and arts, and serves as a council member of the Association for Developing Beijing and Kunqu Operas.

Huang Quanxin has devoted his spare time to the study of calligraphy, paintings and other Chinese traditional culture and arts as well as to the education of arts. Up to now more than thirty of his books have been published, including *Grand View of China's Auspiciousness Series, The Series of Authentic Characters of Fu (fortune), Lu (emoluments), Shou (longevity) and Xi (happiness) by Famous Calligraphers of Past Dynasties, Modern Inscriptions, A Copybook of Ancient Chinese Poems, An Intense Course for Practical Fountain Pen Handwriting*, and *Elementary Handwriting for Young People*. In addition he has been a designer for many books. Huang Quanxin, who enjoys a high reputation in China and abroad, is included in the *Directory of Eminent Literary Personnel of China* by the Research Institute of Literature of the China Academy of Social Sciences.

# Contents

# Chapter I  Wei Stone Inscriptions

## 1. Origin and Development

Wei stone inscriptions, or the stone inscriptions of the Northern Wei (386-534), belong to regular script. Chinese calligraphy reached its great prosperity in the Jin (265-420) and the Southern and Northern dynasties (420-589), an important historical period that formed a connecting link between what preceded and that which followed. Wei stone inscriptions show bold innovation spirit and outstanding creative abilities during the evolution from official script to regular script of the Tang Dynasty (618-907).

## 2. Evolution from Official to Regular Script

Wei stone inscriptions appeared during the transition from official to regular script. The beauty of it lies between likeness and unlikeness, showing both the simplicity and unsophistication of official script and an inkling of regular script of the Tang Dynasty. In the evolution from official to regular script, Wei stone inscriptions were of various styles. Dignified and unadorned, Wei stone inscriptions are characterized by free, easy, elegant and upright forms in varied sizes. Lines are arranged artistically, changes are hidden in neatly written characters and rises abruptly emerge in leveled lines.

## 3. Different Styles

The stone inscriptions of Chinese calligraphy experienced three high tides in the Eastern Han (25-220), Southern and Northern Dynasties (420-589) and the Tang Dynasty (618-907) respectively. Of the preserved stone inscriptions, most were from the Southern and Northern Dynasties, nearly 3,000-4,000 varieties in various sizes, including inscriptions and bas-reliefs on precipices, monuments, statues, tombstone inscriptions, etc. Some are rude and unconstrained, some are intelligent and graceful and the others are seemingly clumsy, but actually artful. In various forms and styles, they are very appealing.

## 4. Natural Wit and Humour

In the Tang Dynasty, regular script developed to its maturity with laws in every possible way. Thanks to its beautifully written strokes, square shape and well-knit structure, regular script was designated as official script.

Wei stone inscriptions were immature regular script with no perfect laws, which gave birth to various styles full of natural wit and interest. In addition, Wei stone inscriptions were usually carved in a rough and slipshod way, thus showing a simple, raw and unsophisticated flavor.

# Chapter II   Techniques of Writing

## 1. Sitting Position

Requirements for one who sits to write:

The head: One should hold the head straight, inclined slightly forward, look at the copybook and keep the mind peaceful.

The body: One should sit straight, keep the shoulders level and the waist stiff, and should not touch the table edge with the chest.

The arms: One should relax one's arms, the left hand resting on the paper and the right hand holding the brush.

The feet: One should rest one's feet parallel on the floor, the legs relaxed and the body stable.

## 2. Standing Position

Requirements for one who stands to write:

Hold the head straight, incline the body slightly forward, look at the copybook and keep the mind peaceful.

Hold the brush with the right hand, place the left hand on the table, and suspend the elbow while writing characters to freely express one's feeling.

Place the right foot slightly forward and the left foot slightly back, and rest the soles flat on the floor with the center of gravity on the right foot.

Write characters with the strength from the waist and the roots of the feet to make every stroke penetrate the paper.

# 3. Holding the Brush

The key points for holding the brush: Fingers are solid, palm relaxed, the wrist parallel, and the palm and brush vertical.

Pushing down: The thumb pushes the brush from inside to outside.

Pressing: The index finger presses the brush from outside to inside.

Hooking: The middle finger pulls the brush from outside on the left to inside on the right.

Squaring: The ring finger pushes the brush from inside on the right to outside on the left.

Supporting: The little finger gives auxiliary strength to the ring finger.

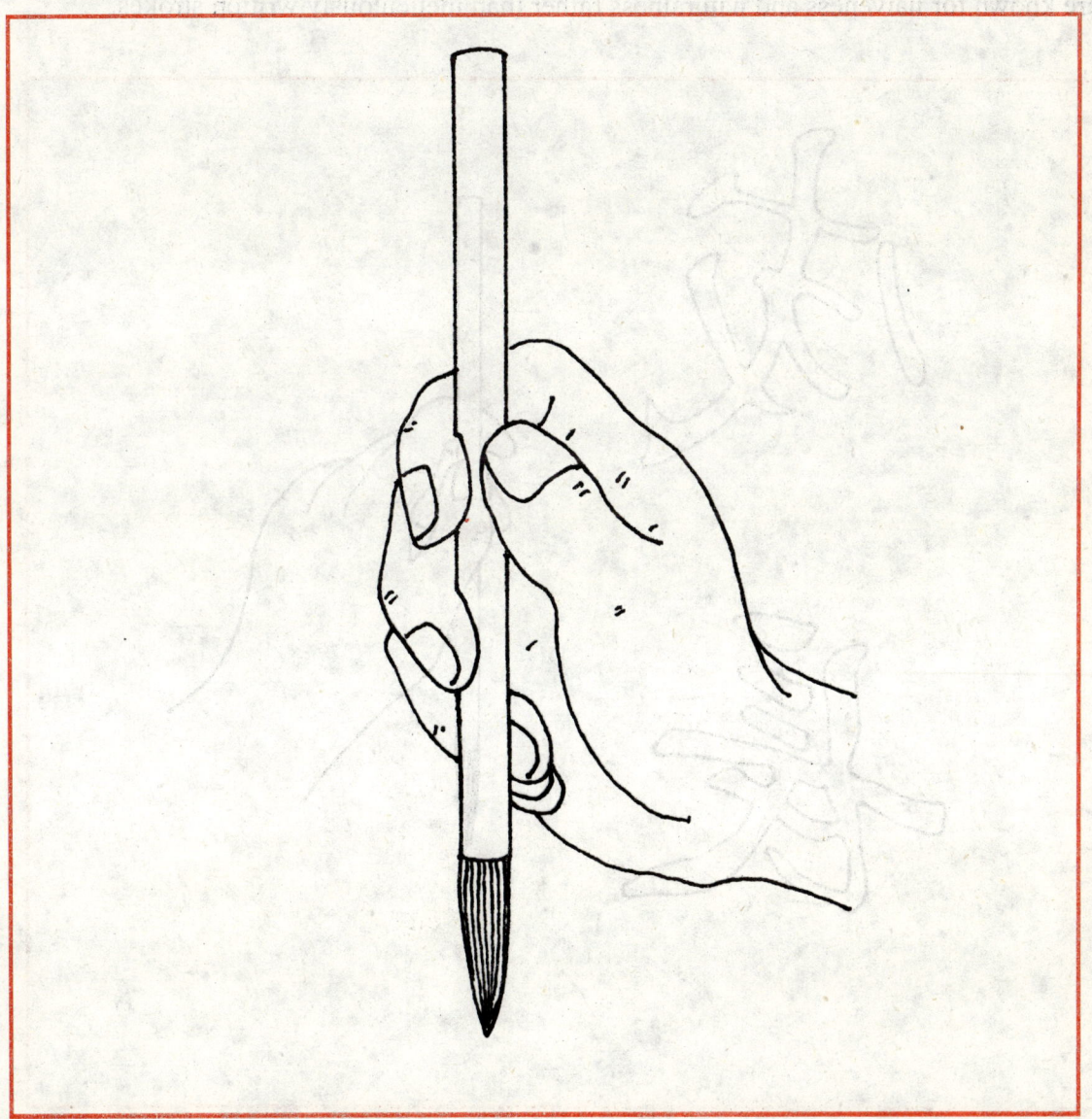

## 4. Movement of the Brush

One should move the brush with the wrist. If the middle point of the brush is used in the movement of the brush, all strength will be concentrated on the brush and strokes will be solid and full of spirit. The contrary-point method is used to start a stroke; the middle-point method, to move the brush on; and the hidden-point method, to close a stroke.

Wei stone inscriptions show characteristics of both official script and regular script. They have sharply rising and falling strokes, the suddenly starting stroke and the rapidly closing stroke, vigorous hooking, rising strokes, and powerful left-falling and right-falling strokes. Cornering strokes in Wei stone inscriptions are square, but the inside is round, made when the brush is tilted to the right. Wei stone inscriptions are known for naiveness and naturalness rather than meticulously written strokes.

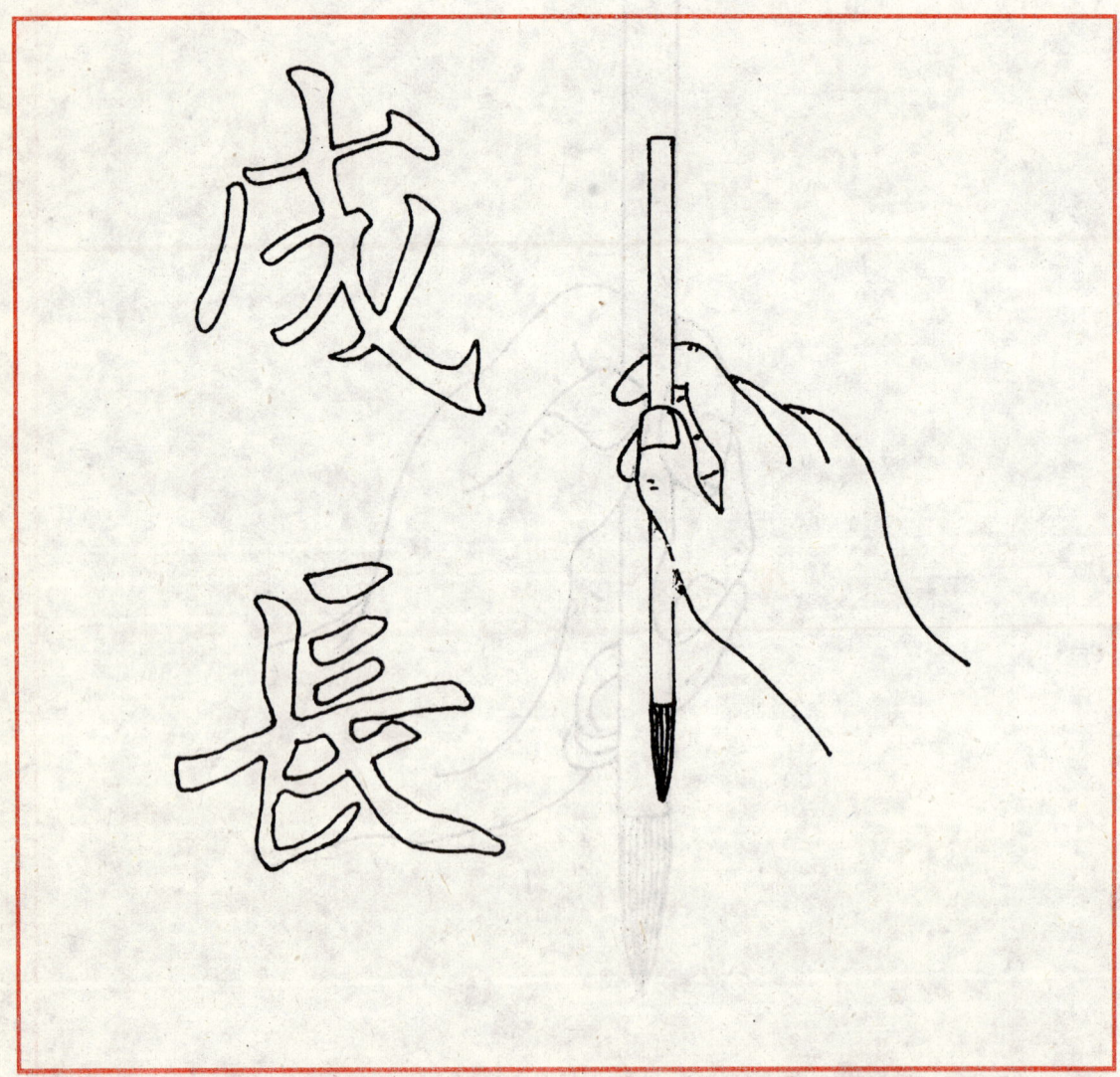

# Chapter III   Strokes

The single movement of the brush is commonly known as one stroke. One who wants to create good calligraphy works must learn to write strokes well.

## 1. Basic Strokes

There are eight kinds of basic strokes: horizontal, vertical, left-falling, right-falling, hooking, rising and cornering strokes and dots.

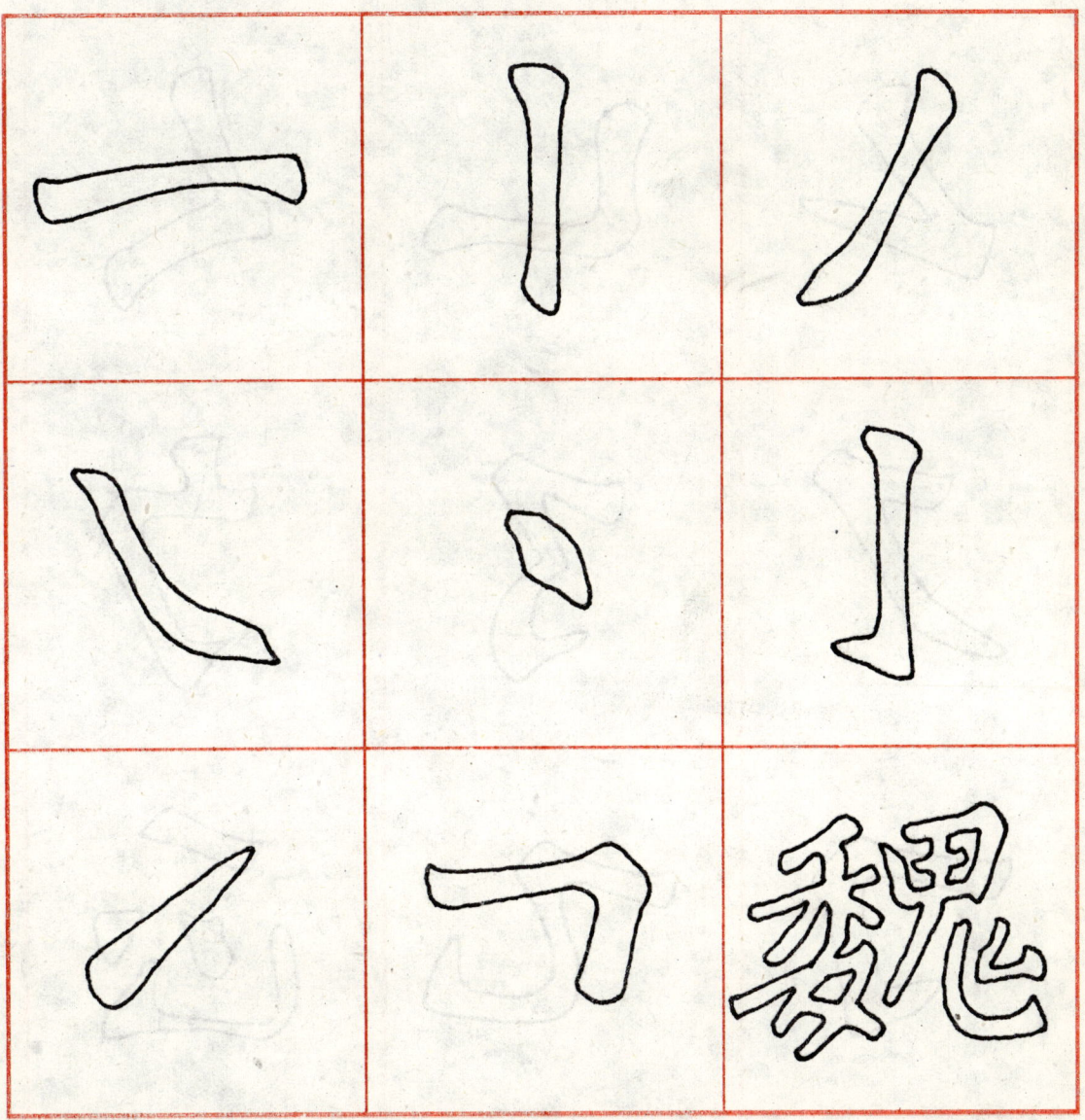

## 2. Complex Strokes

The strokes of Chinese characters are mainly divided into basic strokes and complex strokes. A complex stroke consists of two to three basic strokes. There are eight kinds of basic strokes, and several dozen types of complex strokes.

The following is eight types of complex strokes: left falling-rising, vertical-cornering, left falling-cornering, horizontal-left falling, horizontal-left falling-bending -hooking, vertical-cornering-cornering-hooking, horizontal-cornering-vertical-hooking and horizontal-cornering-bending-hooking.

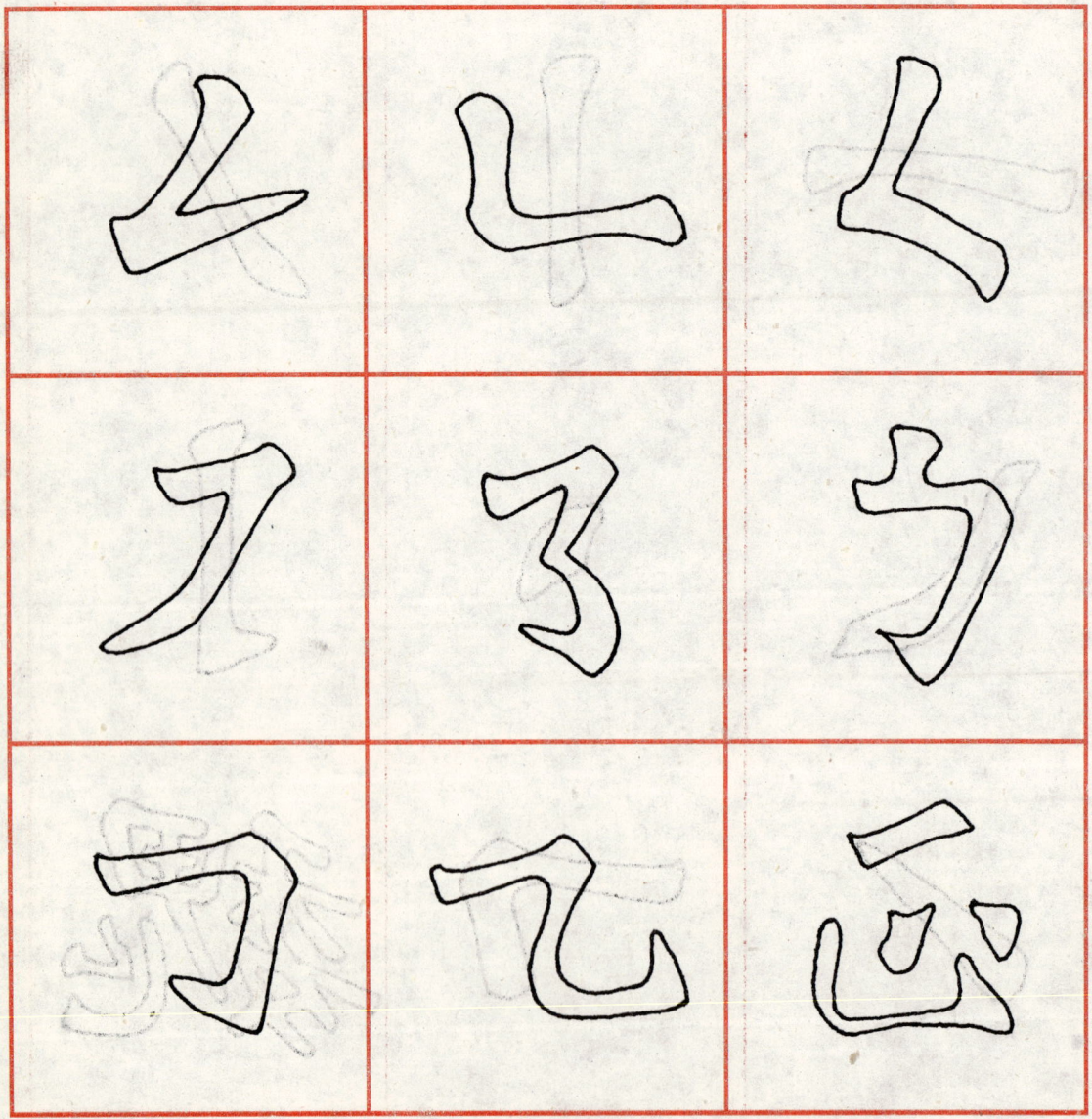

# 3. Eight Sick Strokes

A beginner who is not used to writing with a soft brush is not able to move the brush smoothly, and his ability will fall short of his wishes. More often than not, he or she will produce sick strokes, which our forefathers gave them the names as follows: Bamboo Pool for Carrying Wood, Broken Log, Nail's Top, Upturned Tail, Cattle's Head, Crane's Kneel, Pointed Knife and Edge.

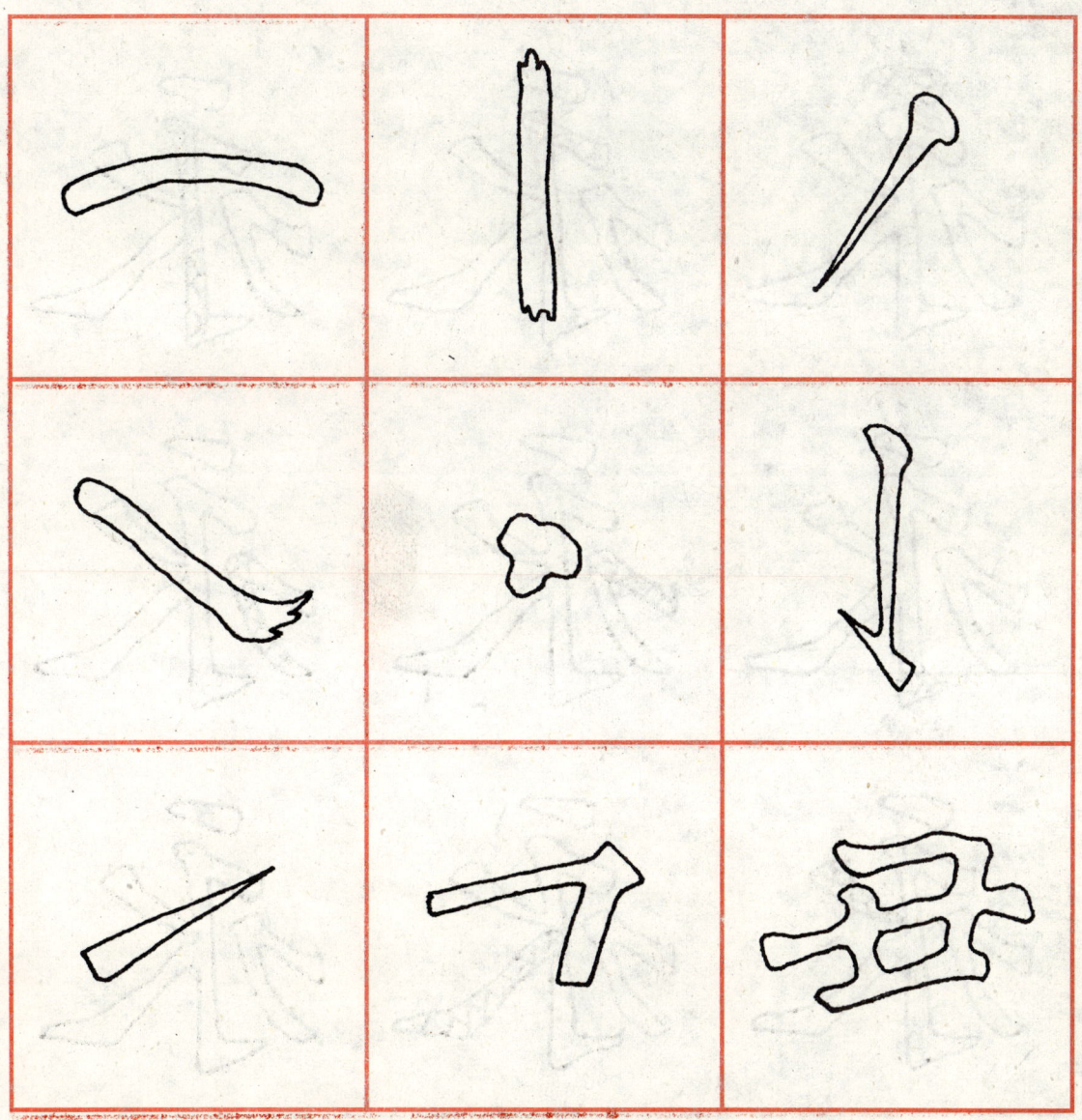

## 4. The Way to Write the Character 永

The way to write the character 永, a method of teaching how to write Chinese characters, has been handed down from ancient times. Legend has it that the way was created by Cai Yong and was later developed by Wang Xizhi. The dot is named Queer Rock; the horizontal stroke, Jade Table; the vertical stroke, Iron Pillar; the hooking stroke, Crab's Leg; the rising stroke, Tiger's Tooth; the left-falling stroke, Rhinoceros' Horn; the short left-falling stroke, Bird's Pecking; and the right-falling stroke, Gold Knife.

# 5. Changes of Strokes

| Different horizontal strokes | 二 | 三 |
| 王 | 班 | 拜 |
| Different vertical strokes | 十 | 中 |
| 昂 | 州 | 順 |

Different left-
falling strokes

Different right-
falling strokes

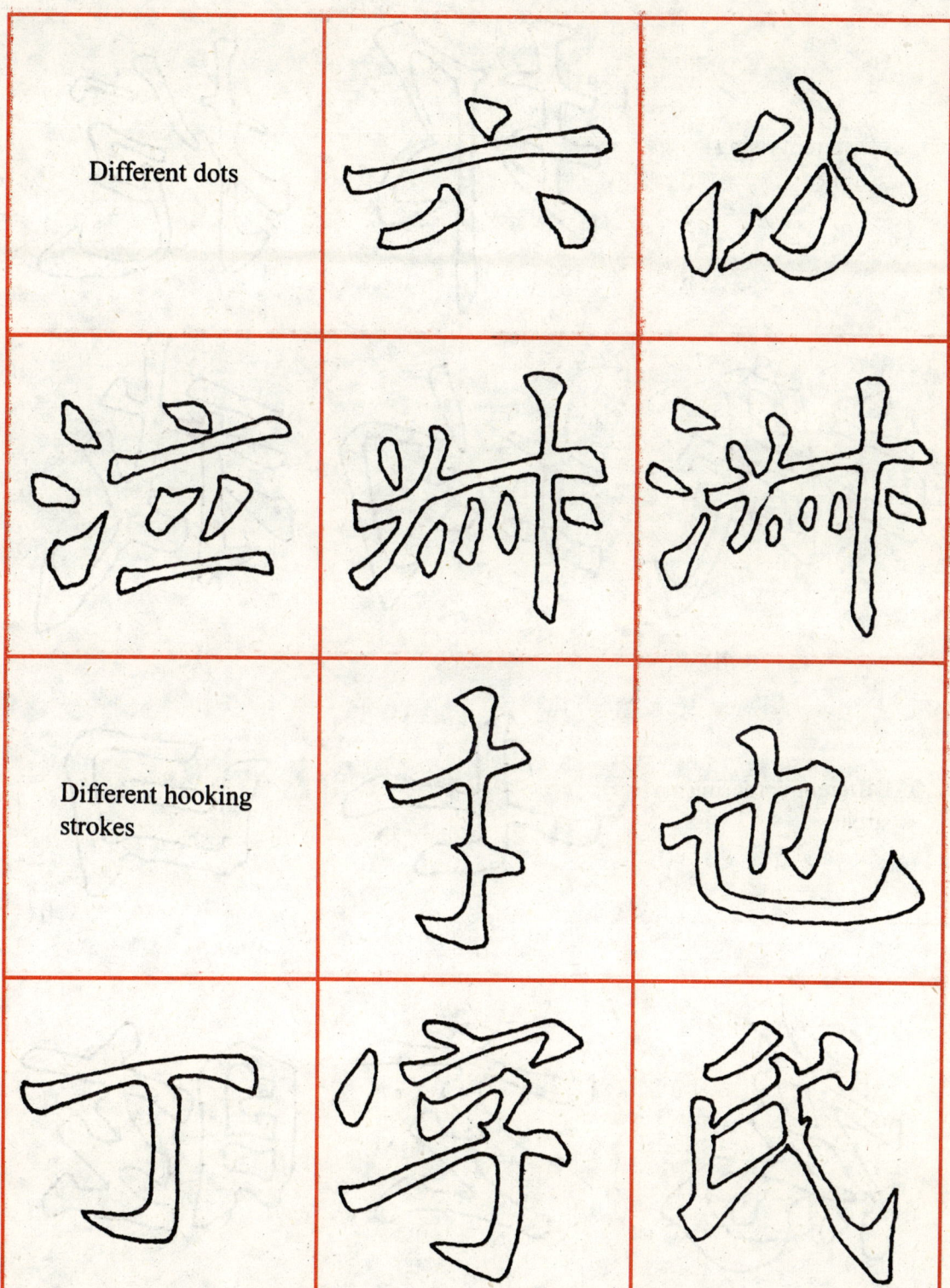

Different dots

Different hooking strokes

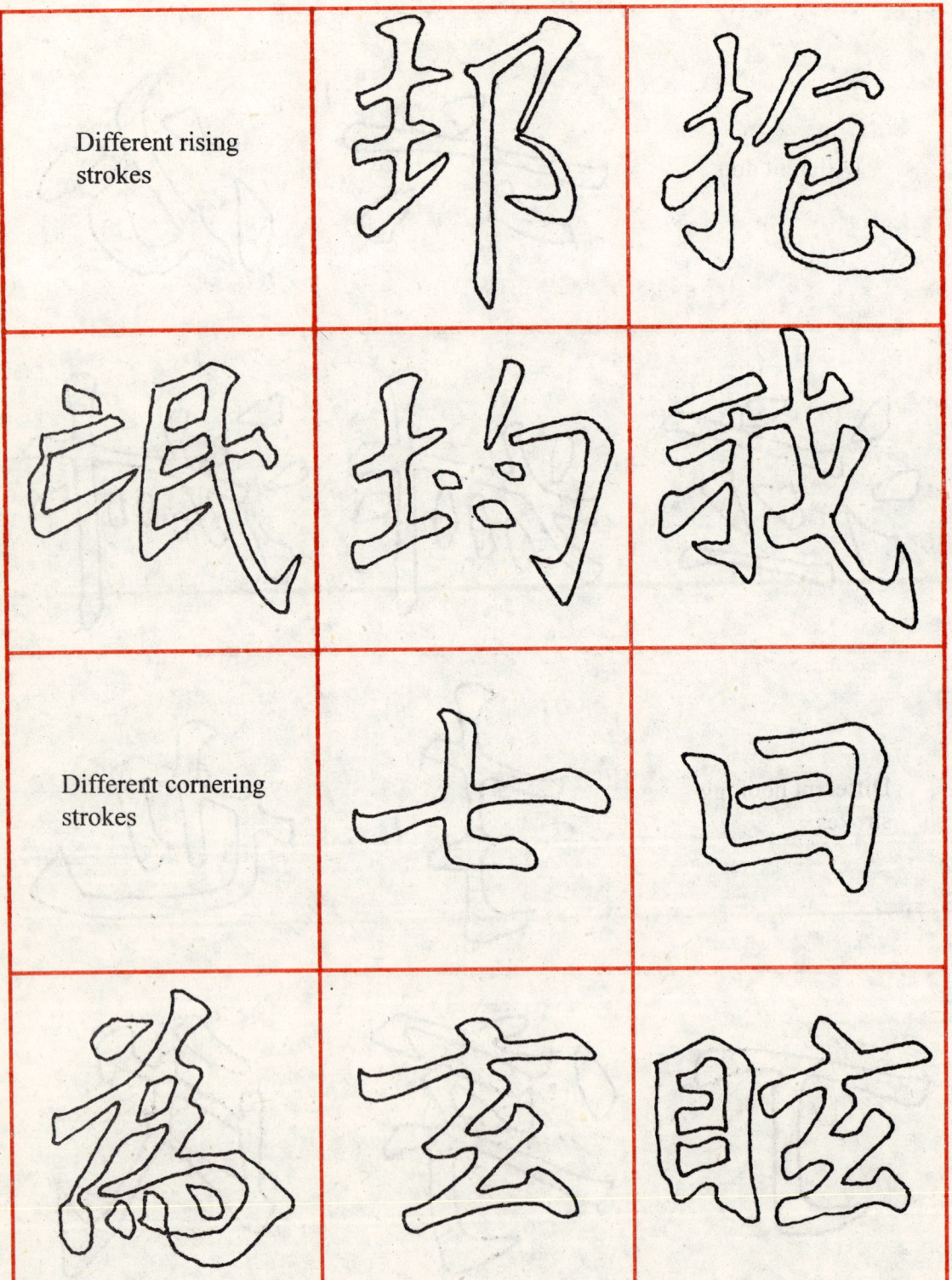

Different rising
strokes

Different cornering
strokes

# 6. Order of Strokes

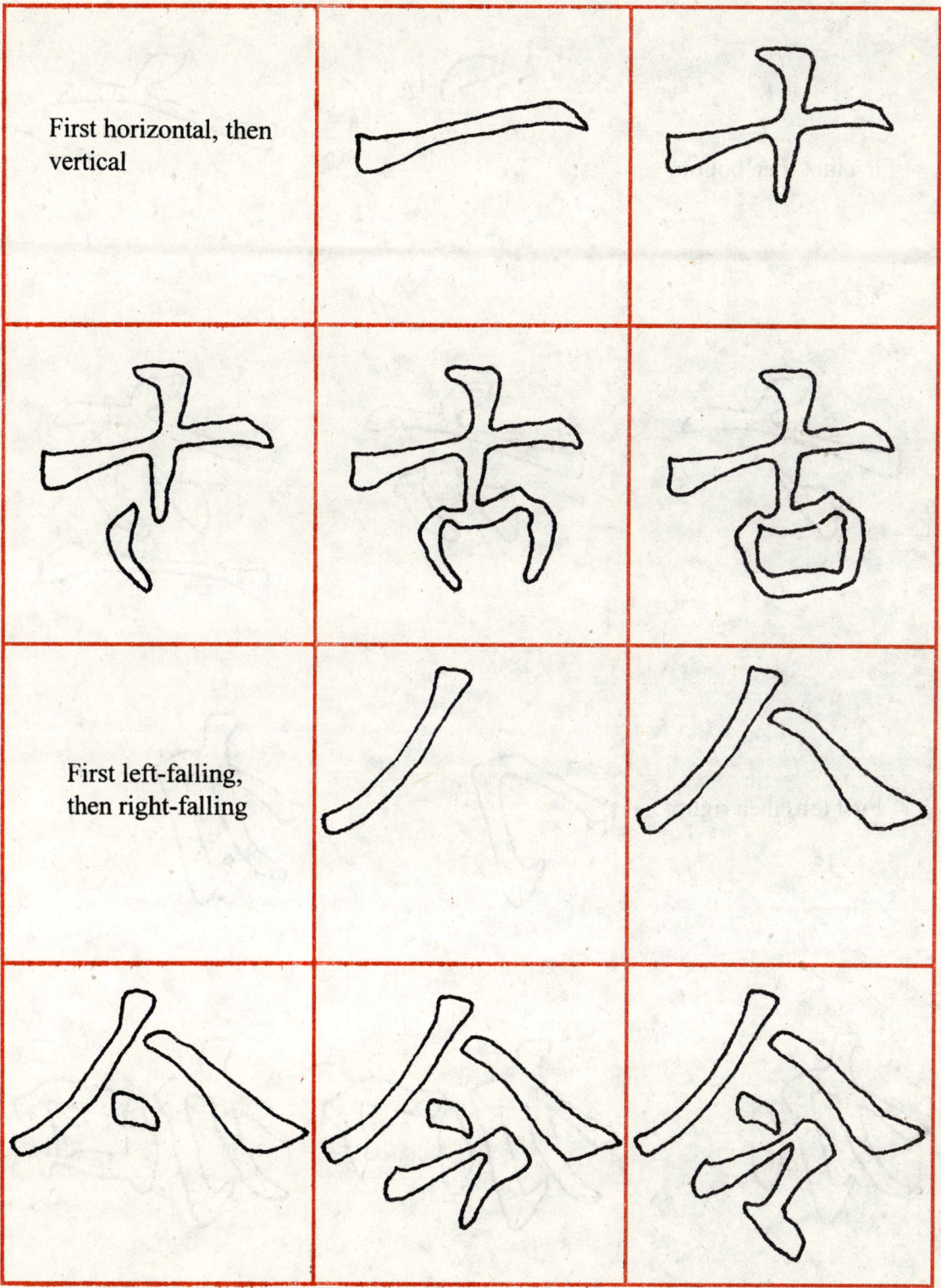

| First horizontal, then vertical | | |
| First left-falling, then right-falling | | |

| | | |
|---|---|---|
| First top, then bottom | 丶 | 亠 |
| 立 | 立 | 立 |
| First left, then right | フ | 力 |
| 力 | 加 | 加 |

First outside, then inside

First inside, then outside

"Let him come in, then close the door."

丶　　丶コ

丶刀　　丶刃　　四

First center, then the sides

一　　二

才　　才　　未

# Chapter IV    Radicals

Side components are the main parts composing compound-element characters. The characters with the same side component belong to the same radical.

More than 90 percent of the Chinese characters are compound-element characters. The number of the characters with the same side component varies from several dozen to several hundred. For instance, there are nearly 600 Chinese characters with the side component of 氵. So if one can write one side component well, it will help in writing well many Chinese characters with the same side component. However, while writing, one must pay attention to the changes of side components.

The radicals are divided into the character's head, character's bottom, left component, right component and character's frame.

## 1. Character's Head

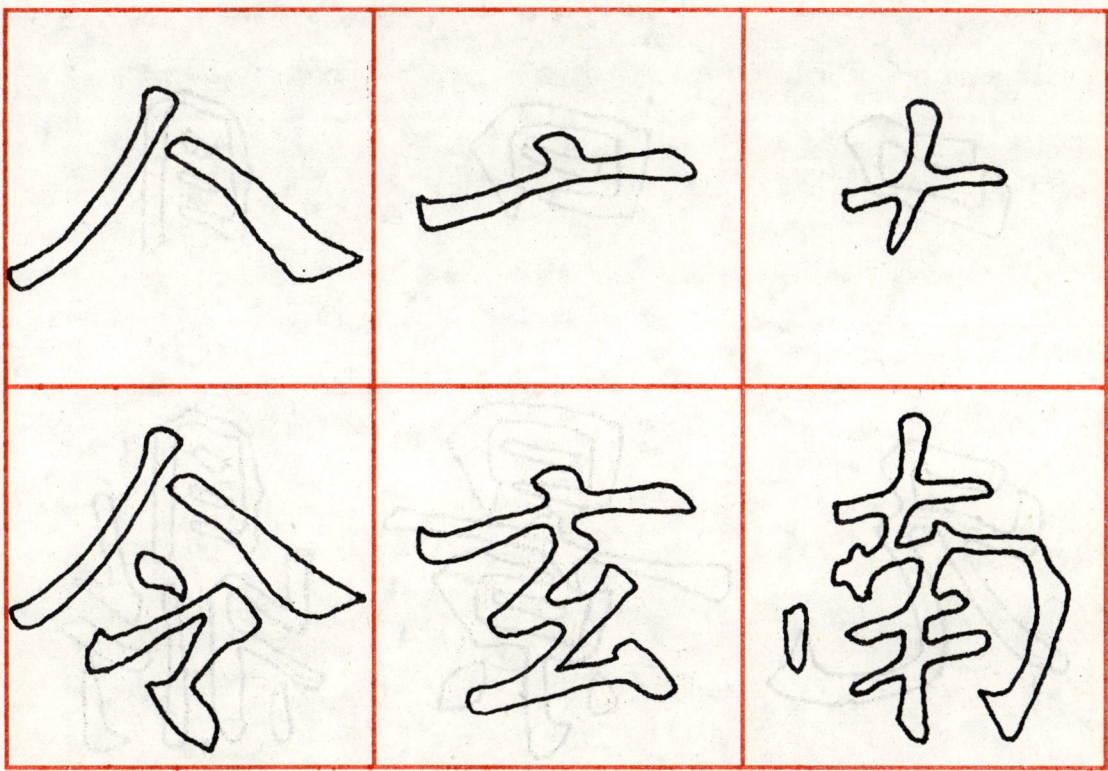

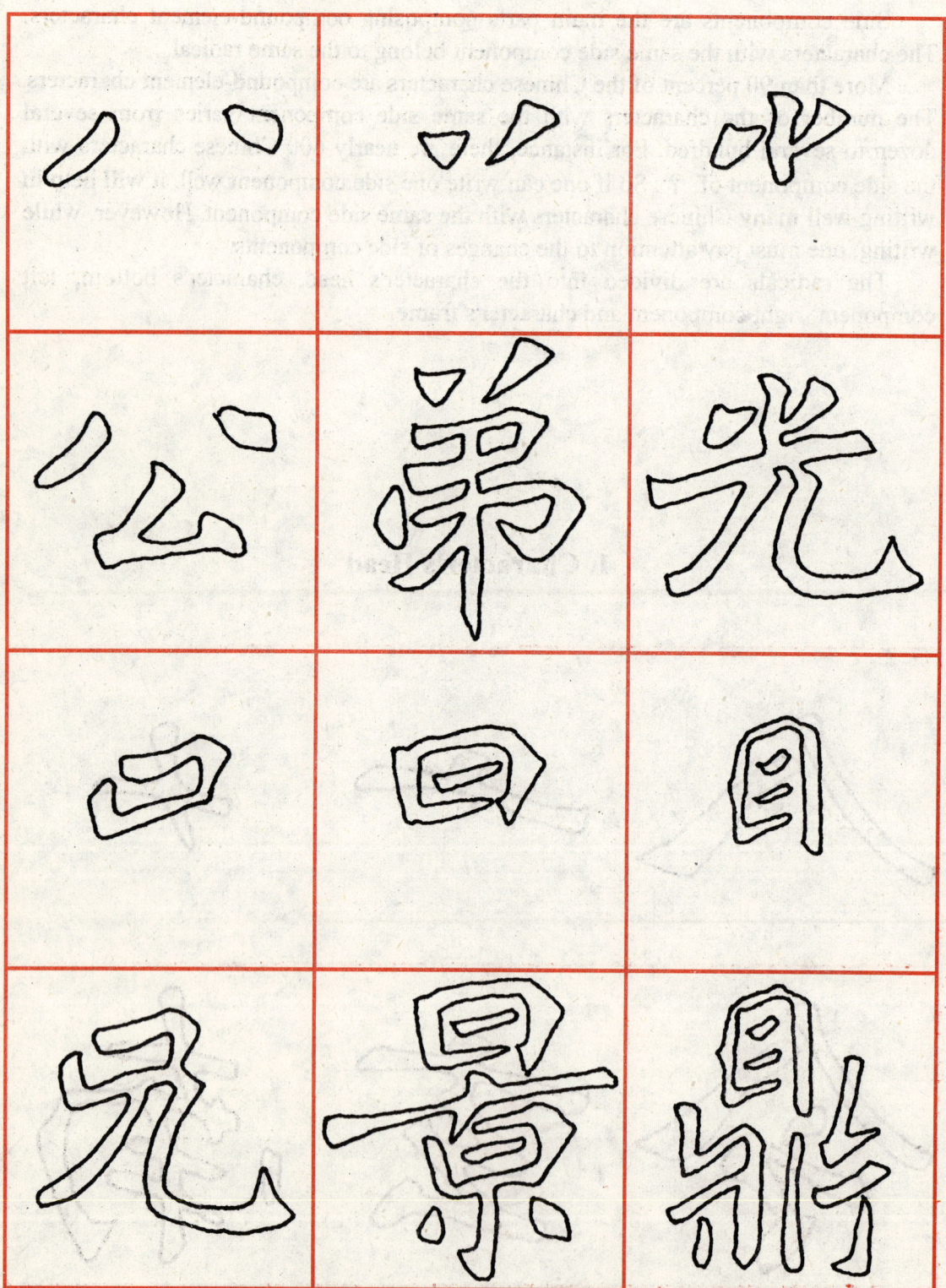

广　广　疒

有　庶　疾

尸　户　步

居　扁　者

山　未　雲

芶　李　雲

坒　走　飛

善　走　登

| | | |
|---|---|---|
| 書 | 春 | 气 |
| 書 | 春 | 氣 |
| 山 | 戈 | 戋 |
| 常 | 戌 | 載 |

## 2. Character's Bottom

| | | |
|---|---|---|
| 王 | 土 | 旦 |
| 皇 | 基 | 暨 |
| 水 | 灬 | 山 |
| 泉 | 然 | 岳 |

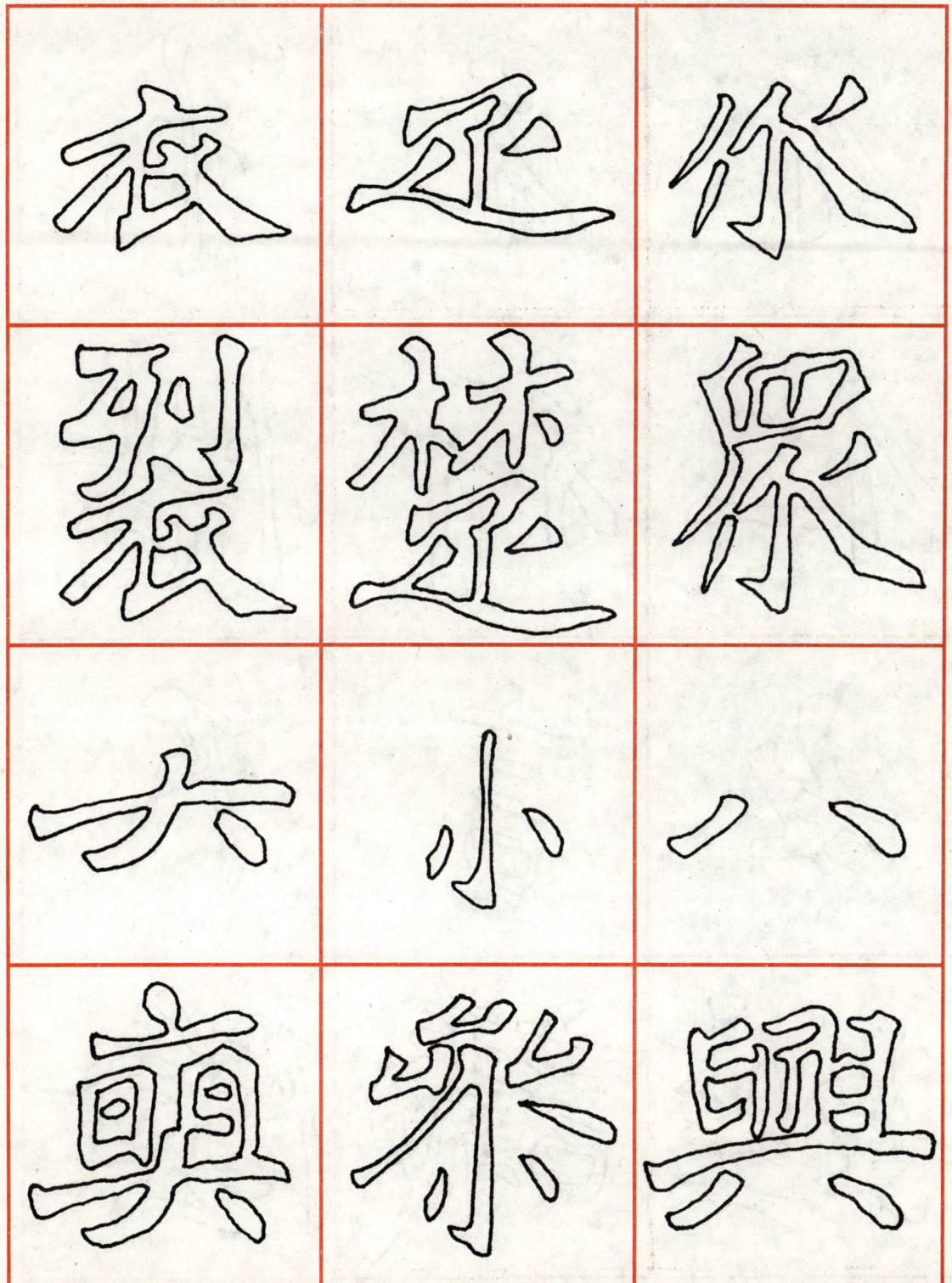

衣 延 你

裂 楚 眾

六 小 八

真 眾 興

冫 亠 爿

次 汚 将

土 玉 十

城 璜 博

## 4. Right Component

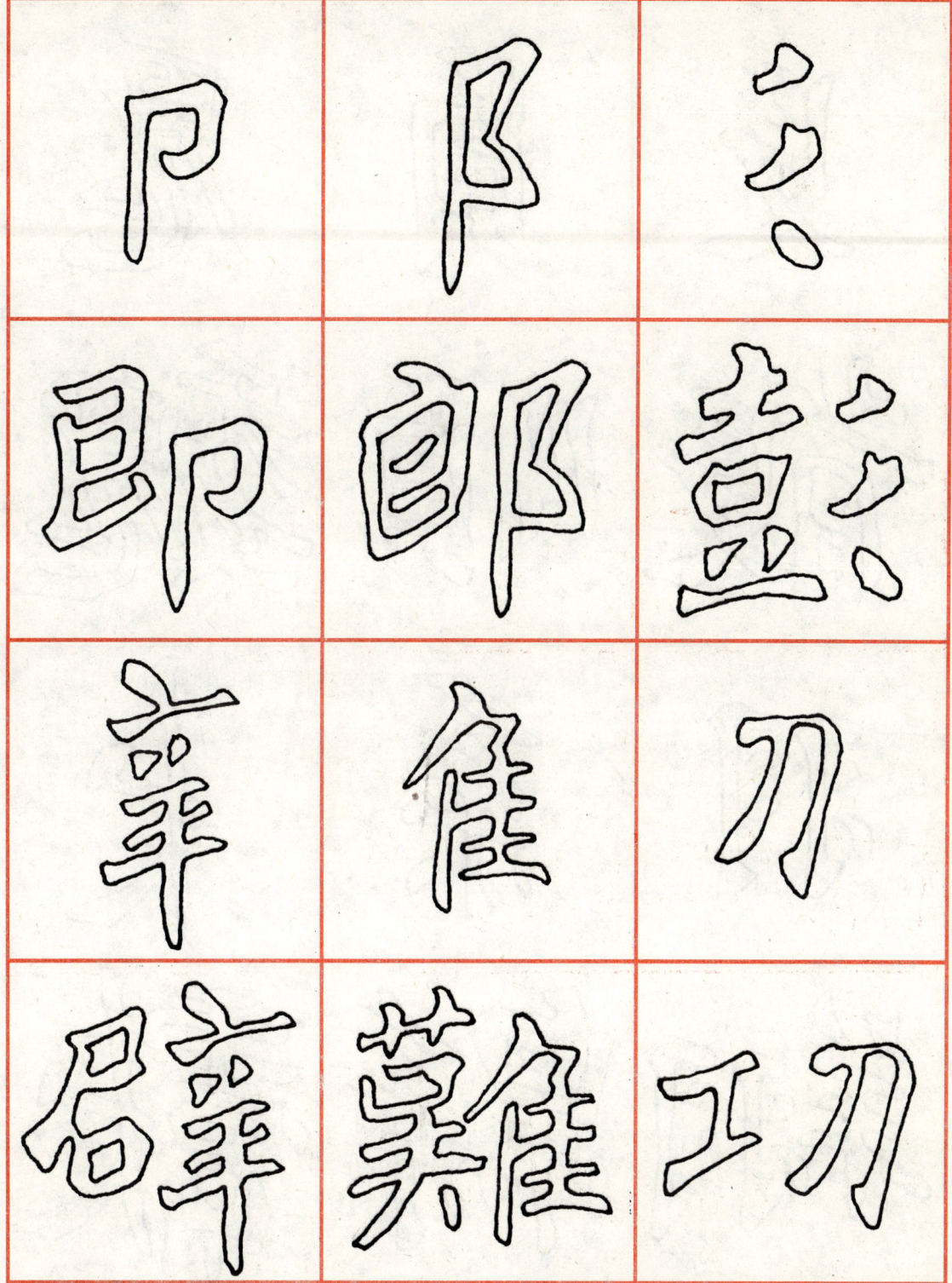

## 5. Character's Frame

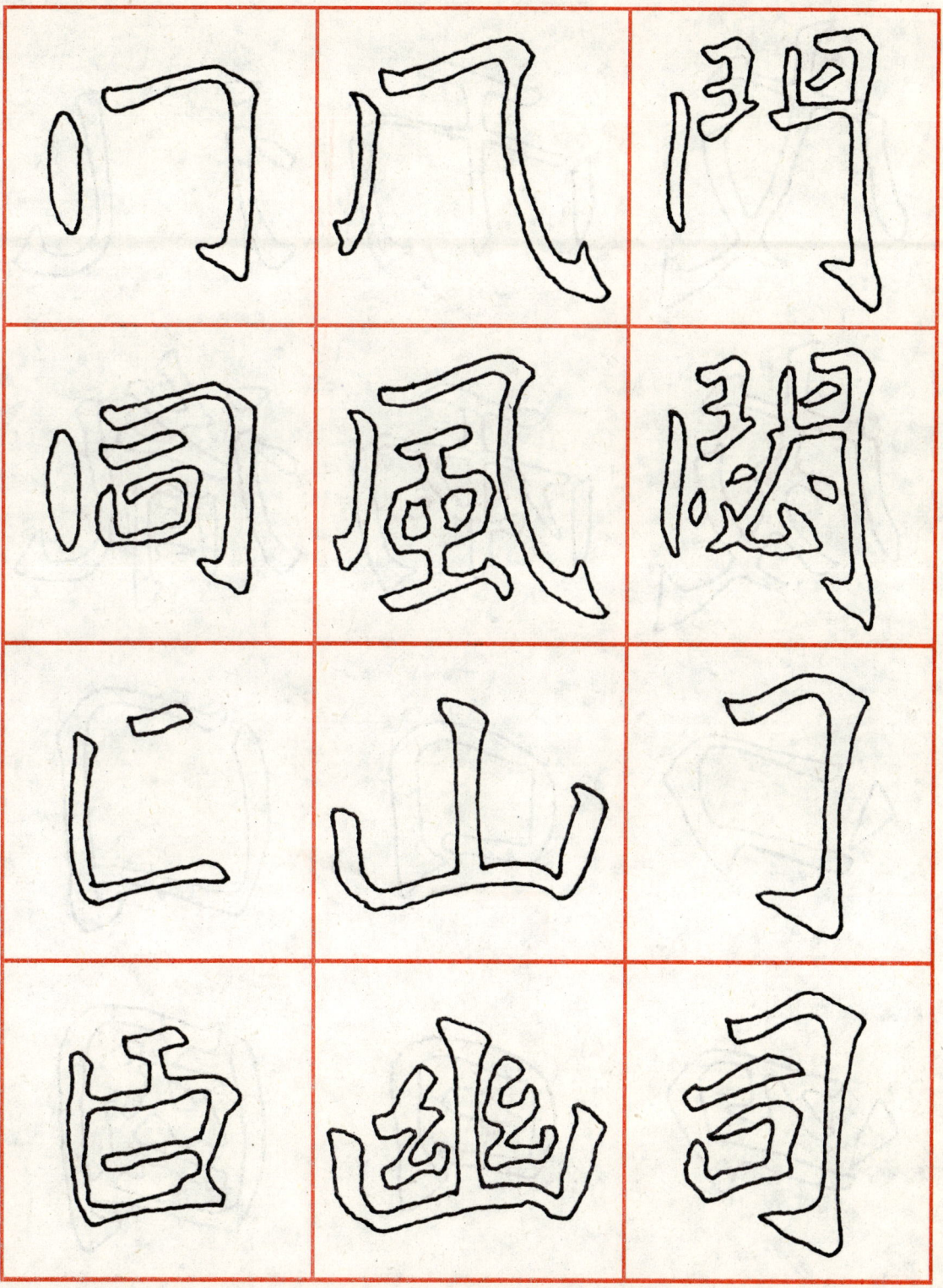

## 6. Changes

|  |  |  |
|:---:|:---:|:---:|
| 宀 | 宀 | 宗 |
| 安 | 守 | 宗 |
| 宀 | 宀 | 宀 |
| 宗 | 宣 | 守 |

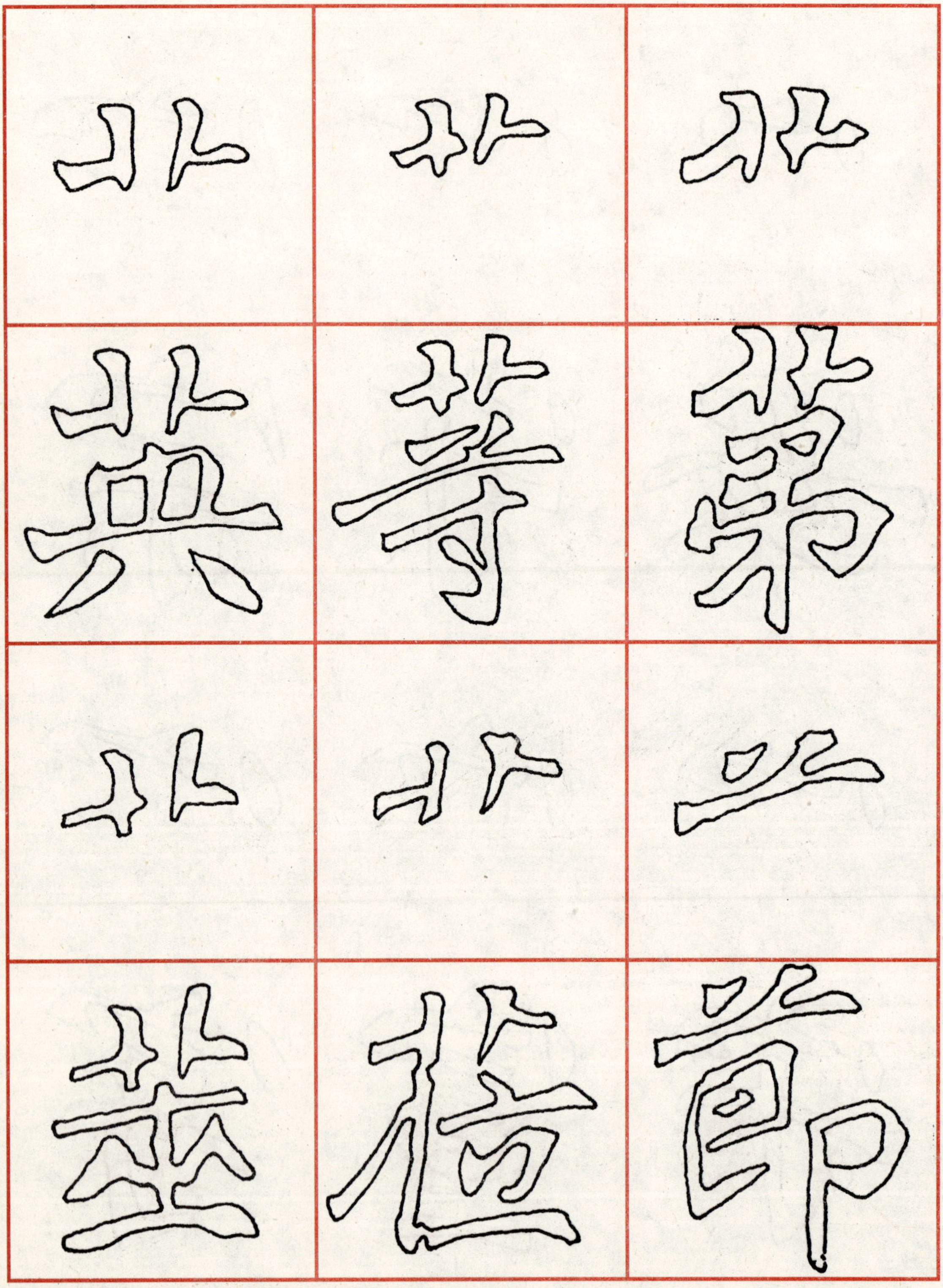
英
等
第
節

| | | |
|---|---|---|
| 艸 | 艸 | 艸 |
| 藏 | 暮 | 蓄 |
| 艸 | 艸 | 艸 |
| 蔫 | 慕 | 恭 |

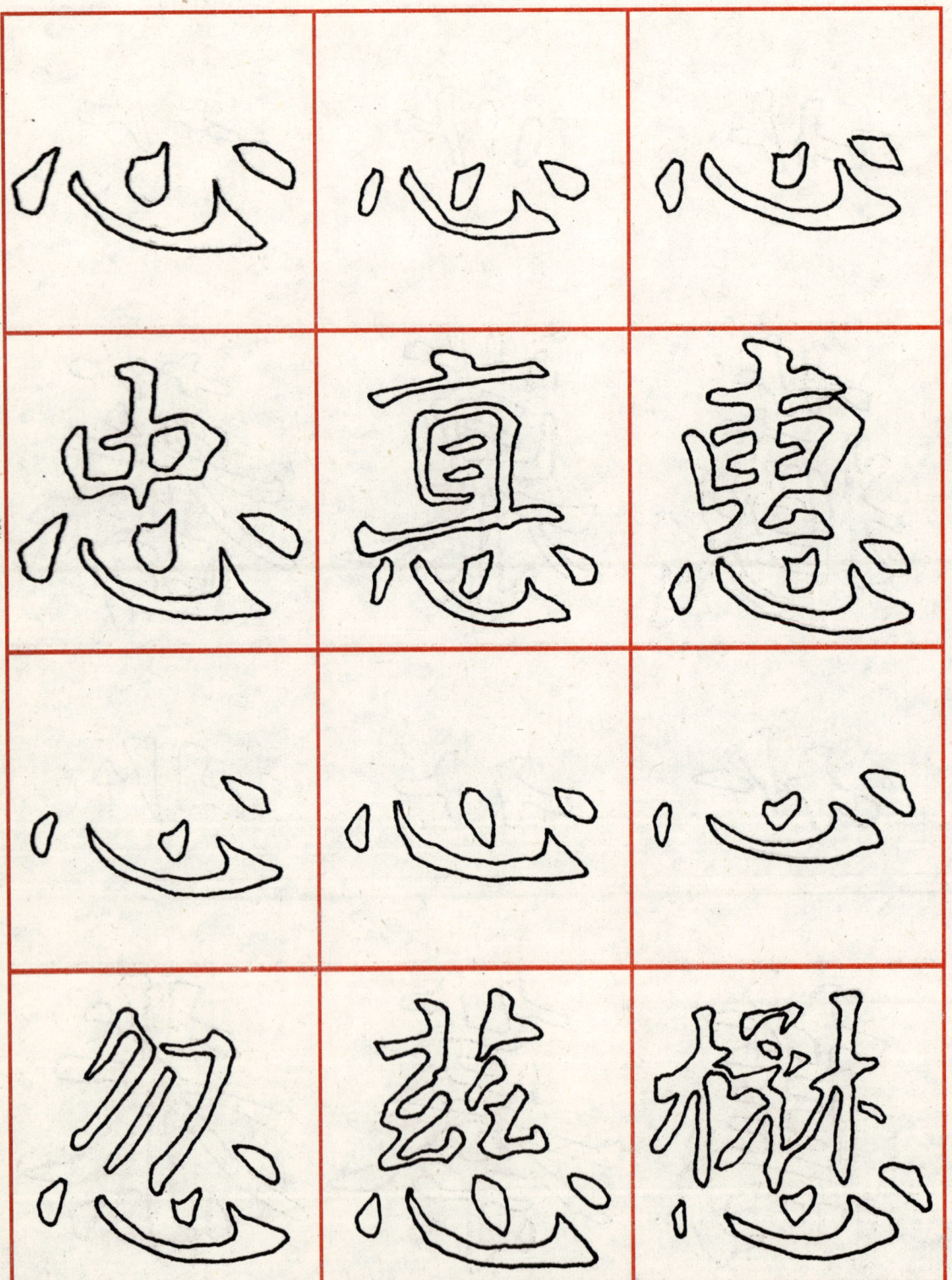

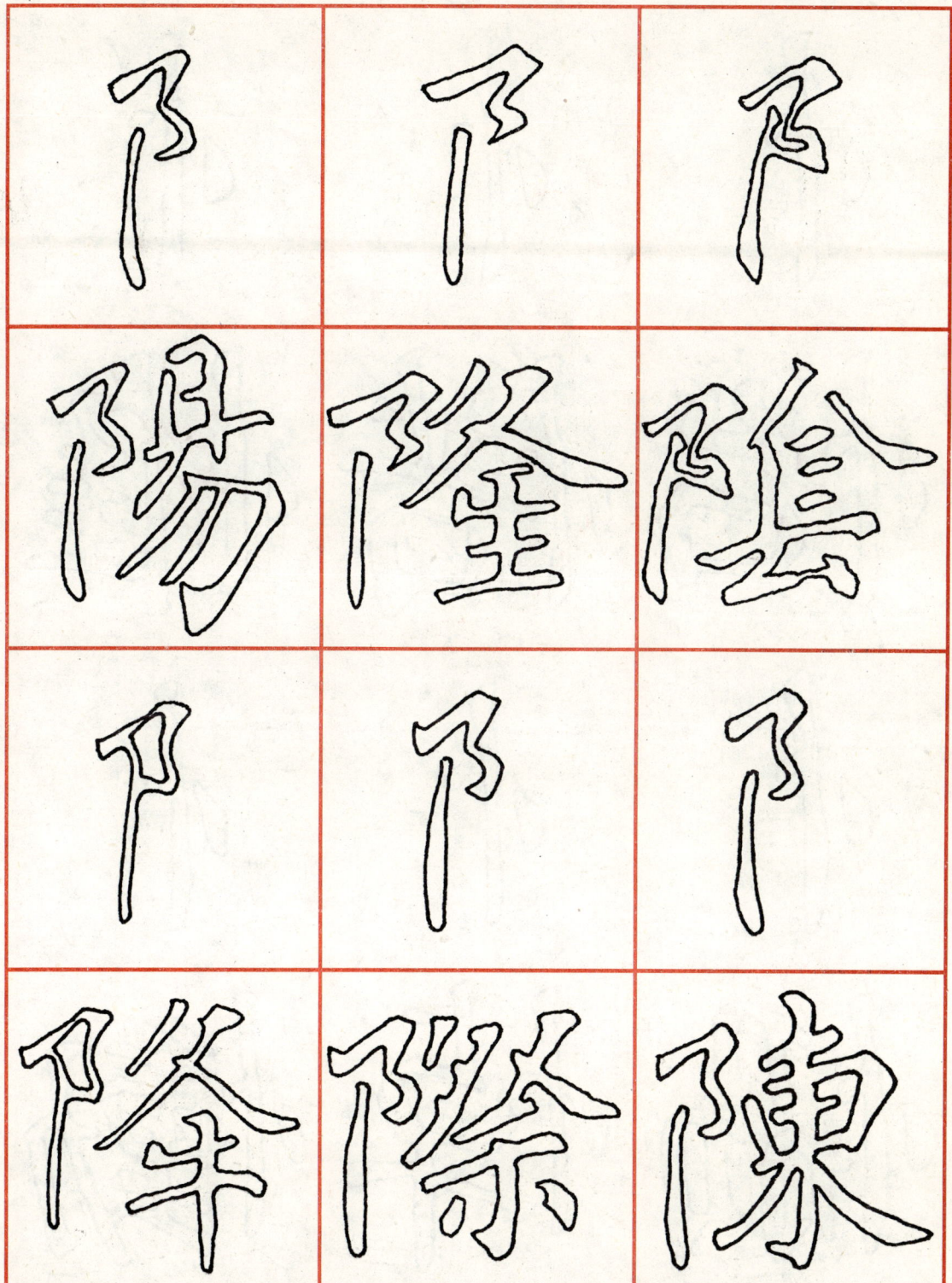

忄

怡　惜　惟

忖　小　忄

協　悼　懃

| | | |
|---|---|---|
| 才 | 术 | 朮 |
| 楊 | 松 | 相 |
| 朮 | 朮 | 朮 |
| 桻 | 樞 | 榆 |

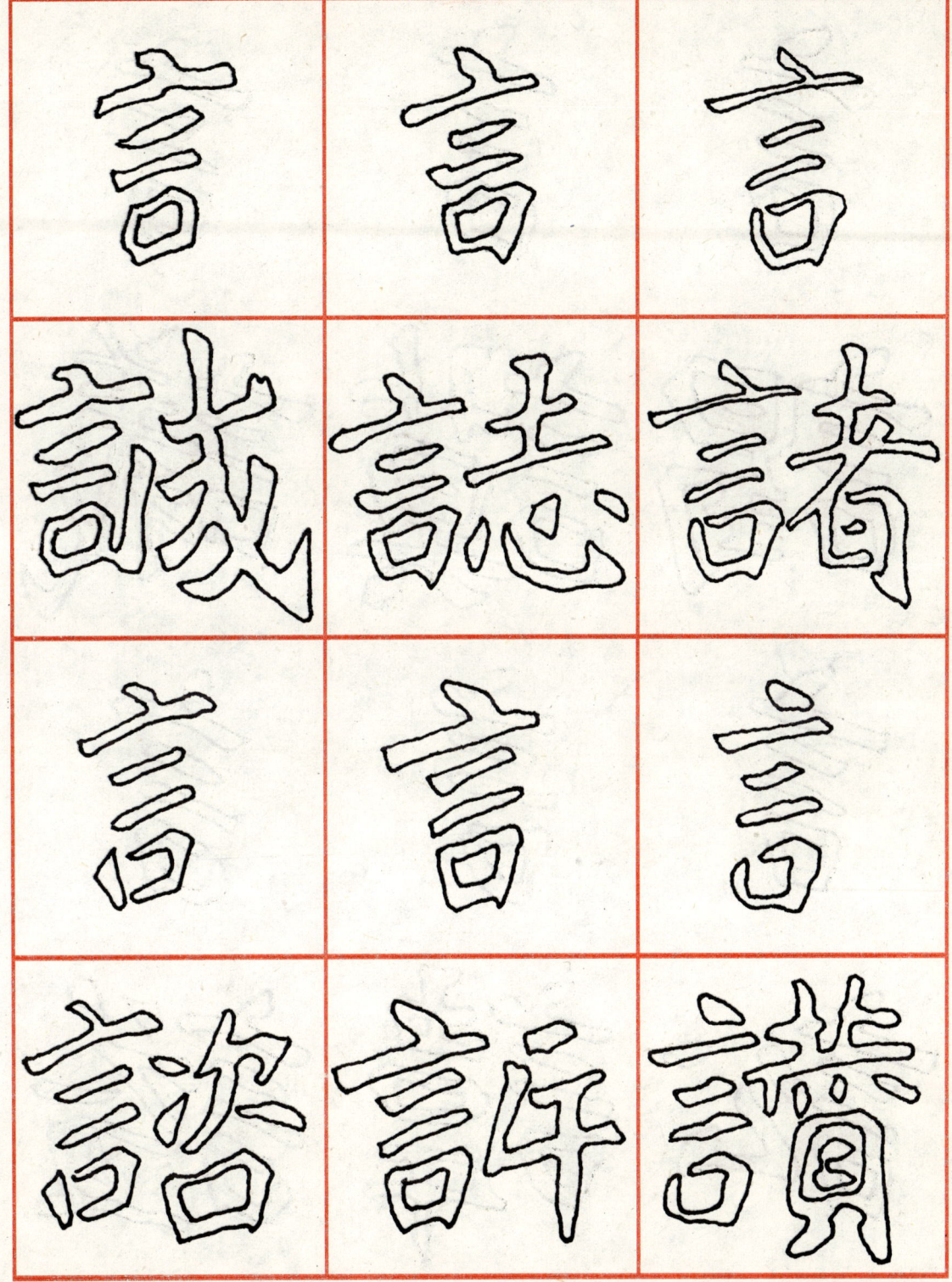

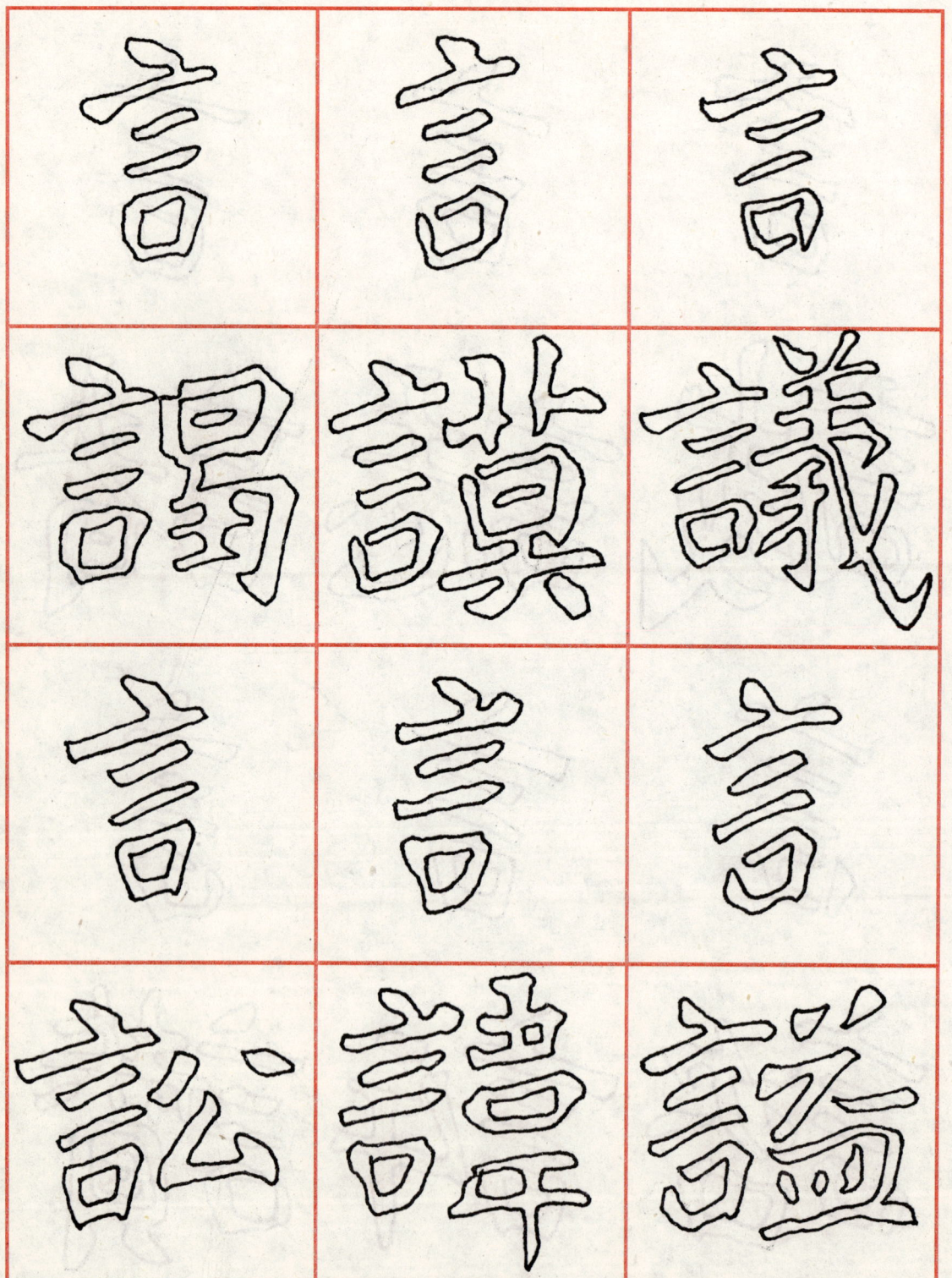

| | | |
|---|---|---|
| 氵 | 氵 | 氵 |
| 清 | 治 | 洛 |
| 氵 | 氵 | 氵 |
| 流 | 汚 | 浴 |

氵 氵 氵

氵 江 波 深

氵 氵 氵

泊 池 淋

氵 氵 氵

温 海 河

氵 氵 氵

泣 淵 滞

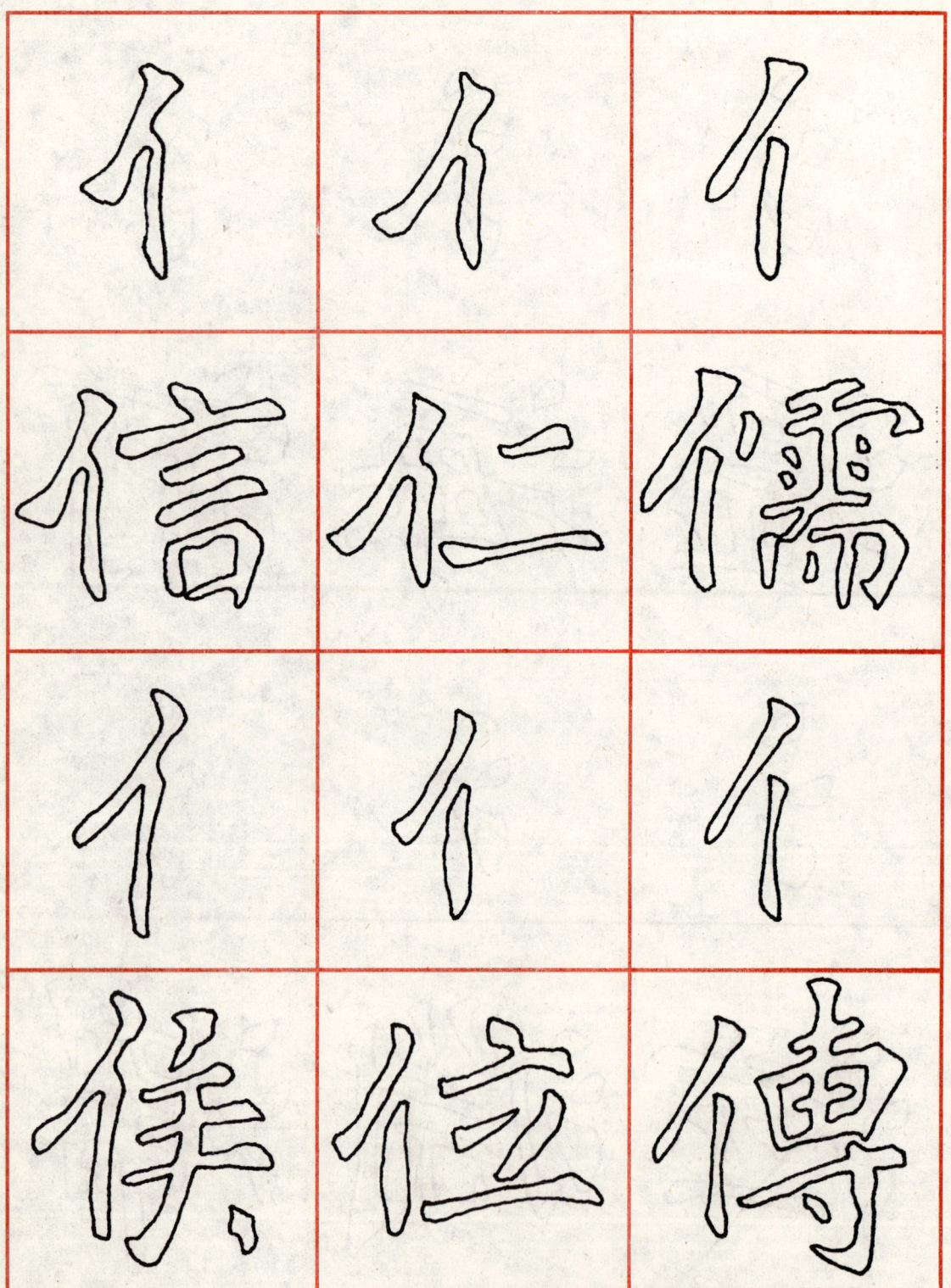

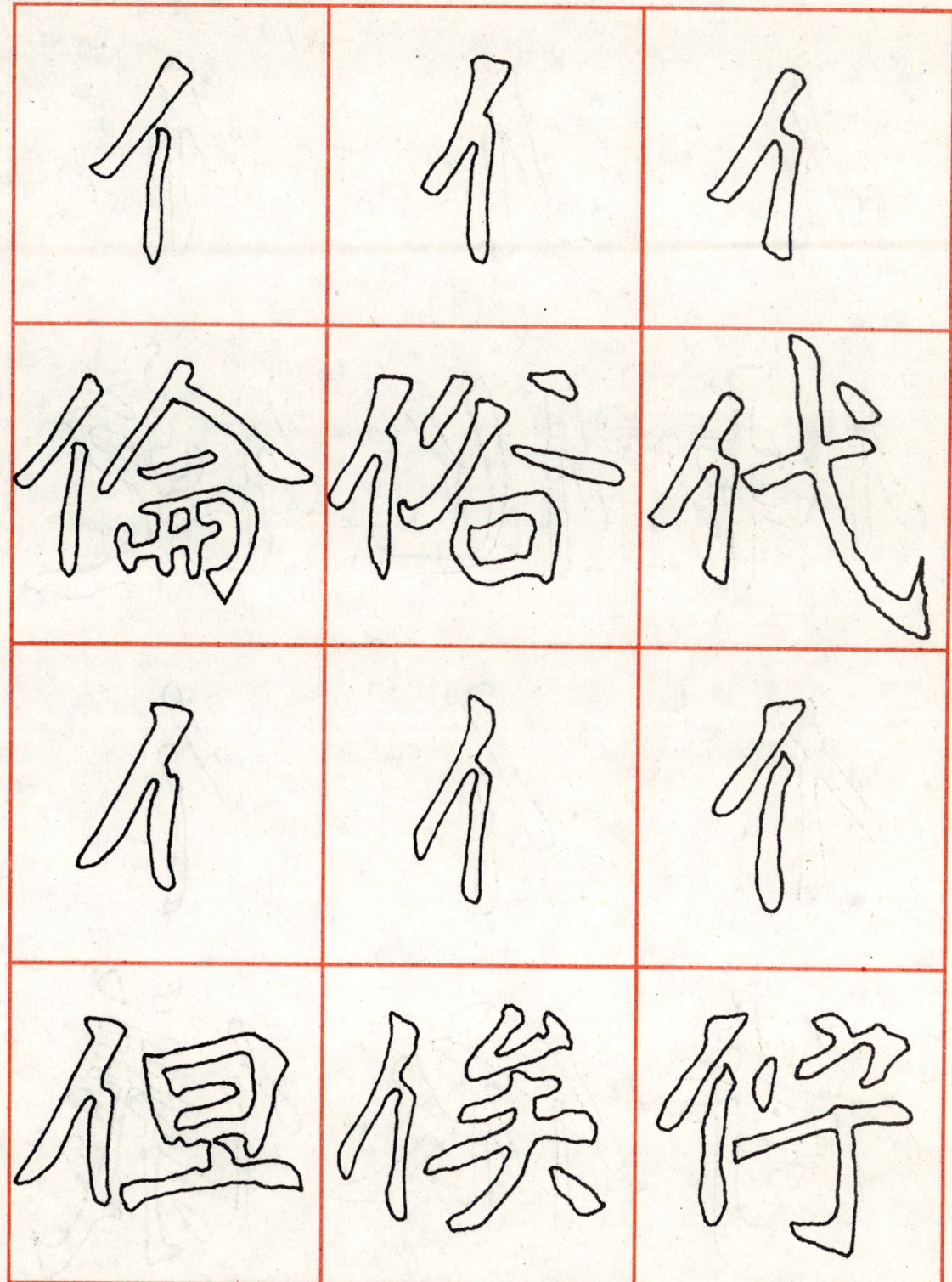

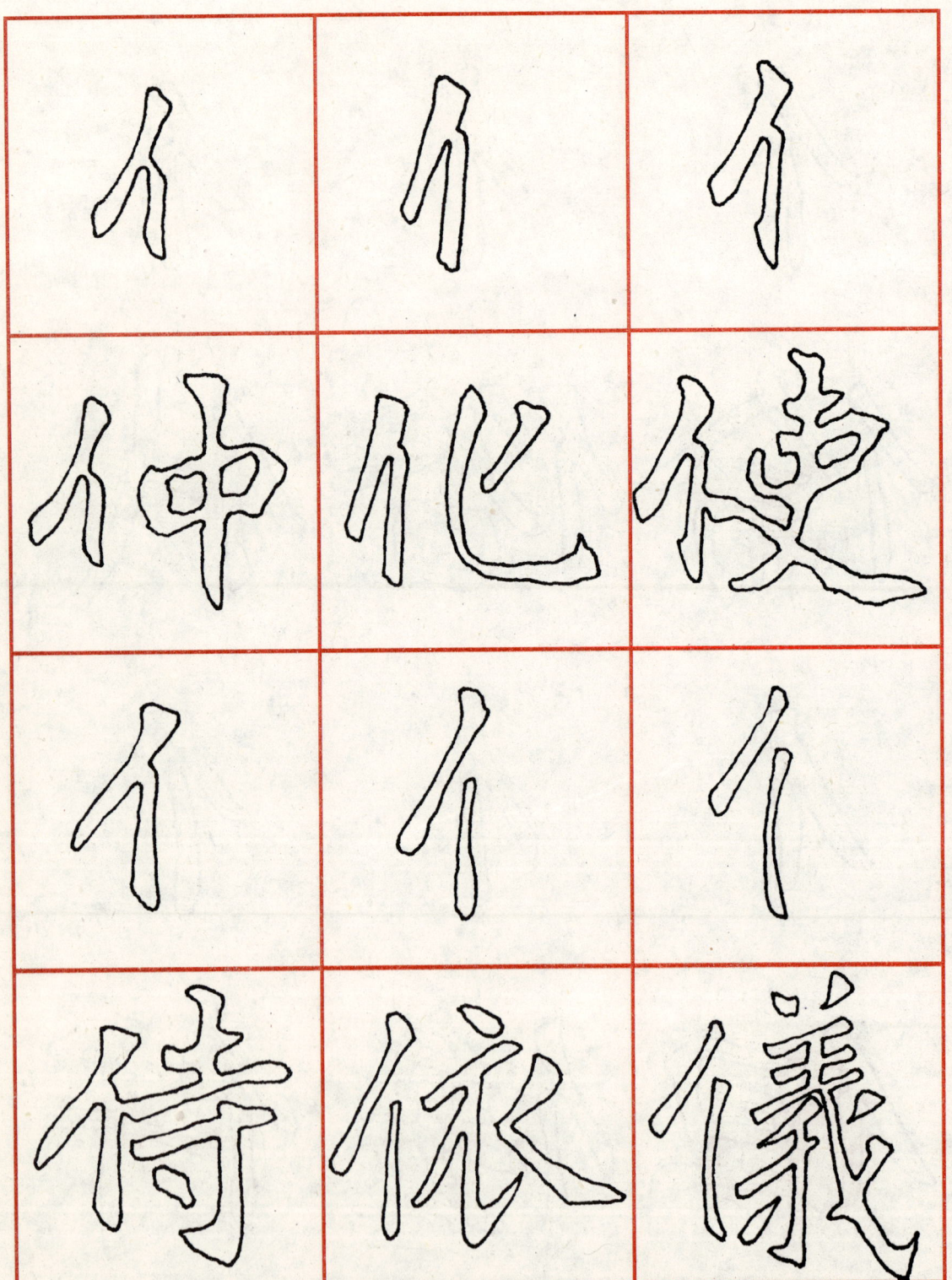

亻 亻 亻

便 仰 傾

亻 亻 亻

隽 僵 俄

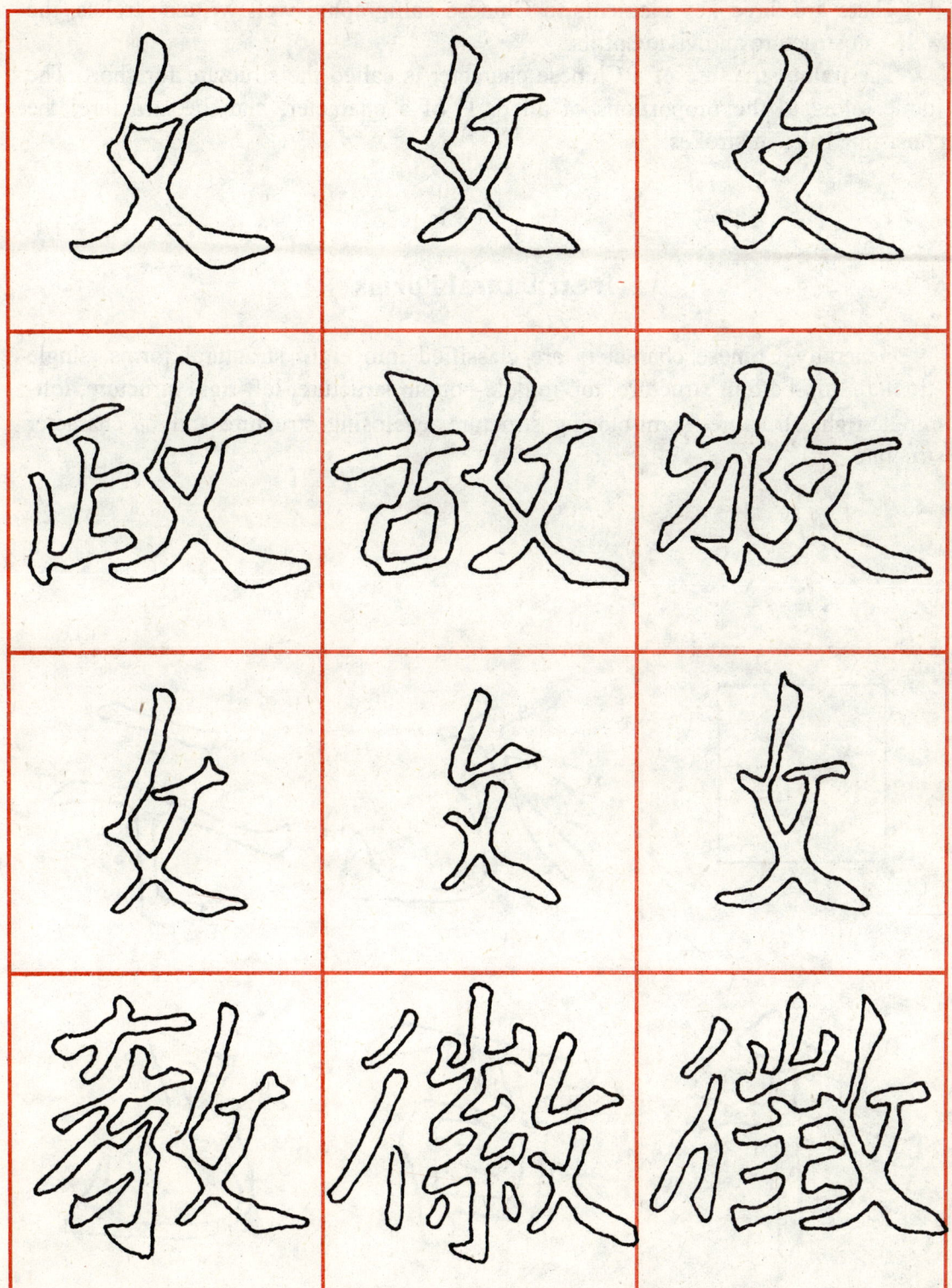

# Chapter VI    Structure

There are three key elements to Chinese calligraphy: well written strokes, the well-knit structure and vivid spirits.

The frame structure of a Chinese character is called the structure for short. The frame refers to the proportions of all parts of a character; and the structure, the consisting rules of strokes.

## 1. Structural Forms

Generally Chinese characters are classified into eight structural forms: single structure, top-bottom structure, top-middle-bottom structure, left-right structure, left-middle-right structure, semi-closing structure, enclosing structure and 品-character structure.

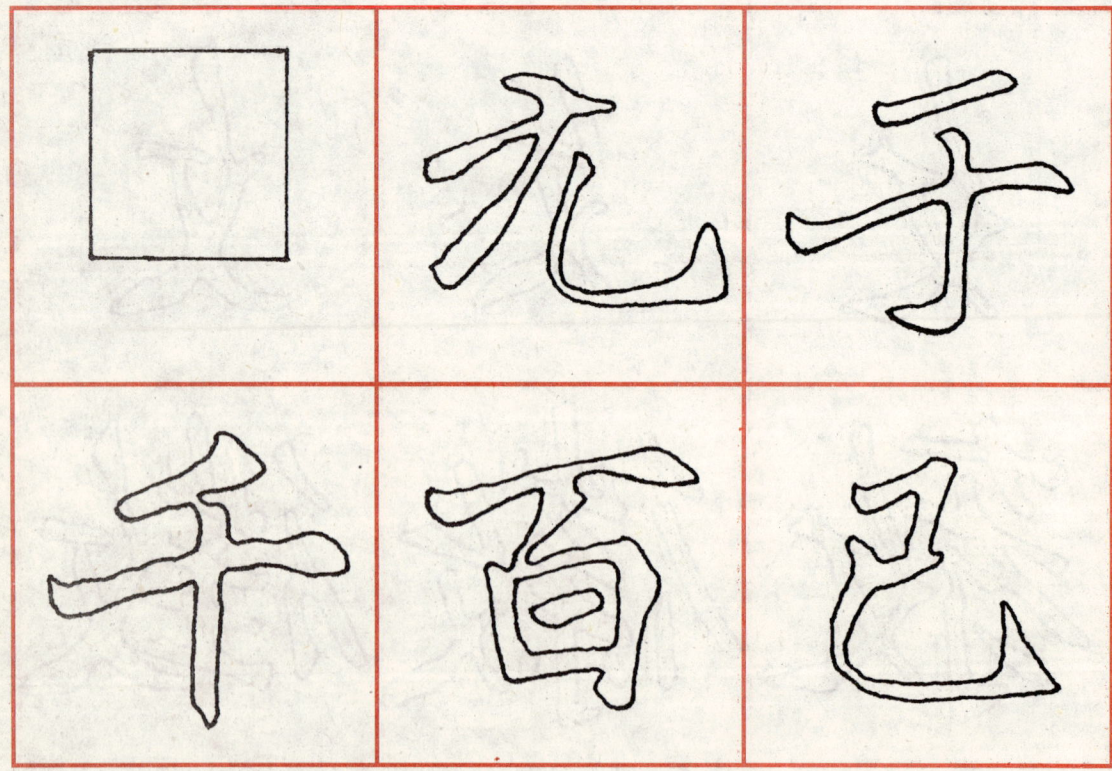

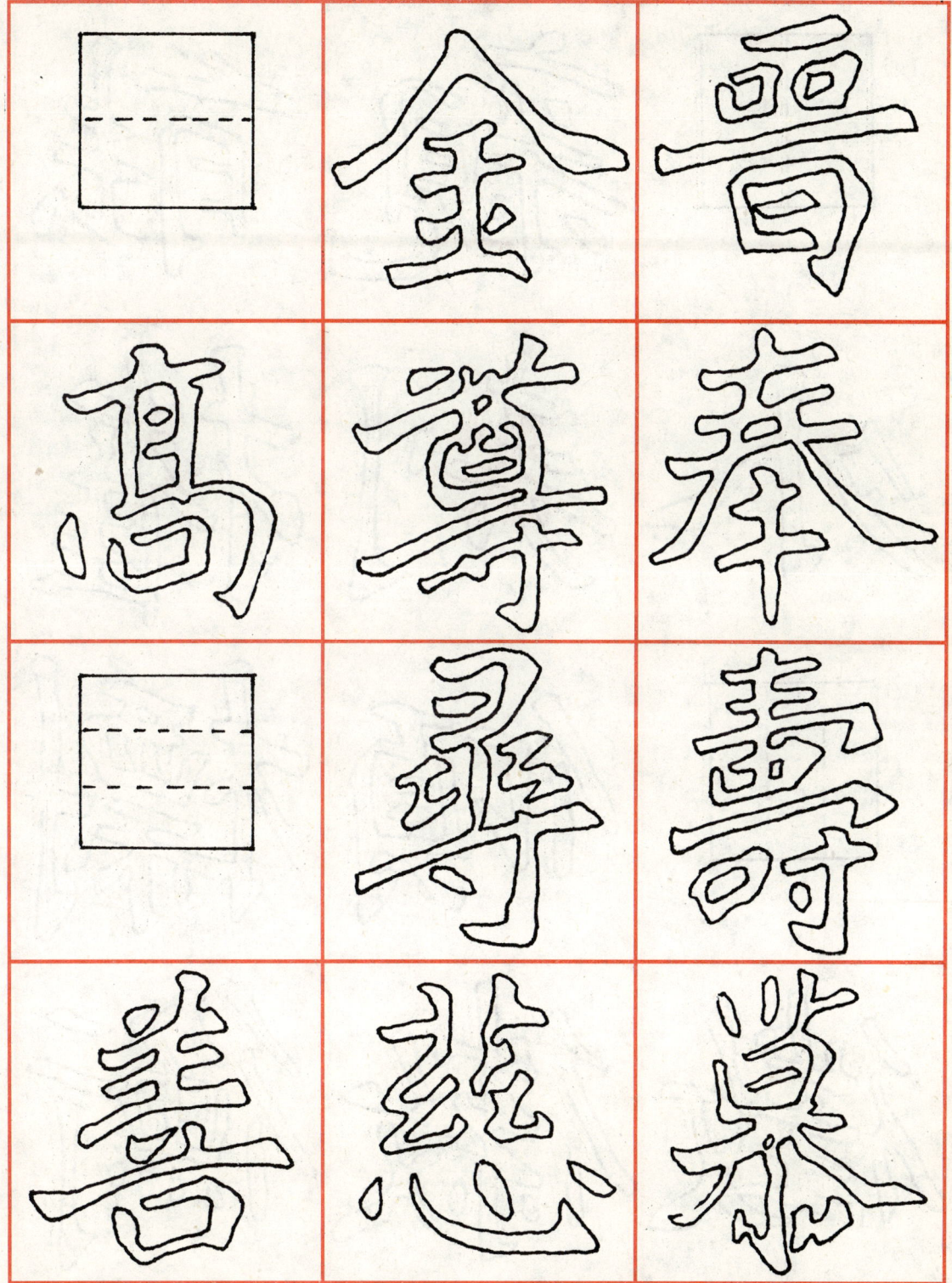

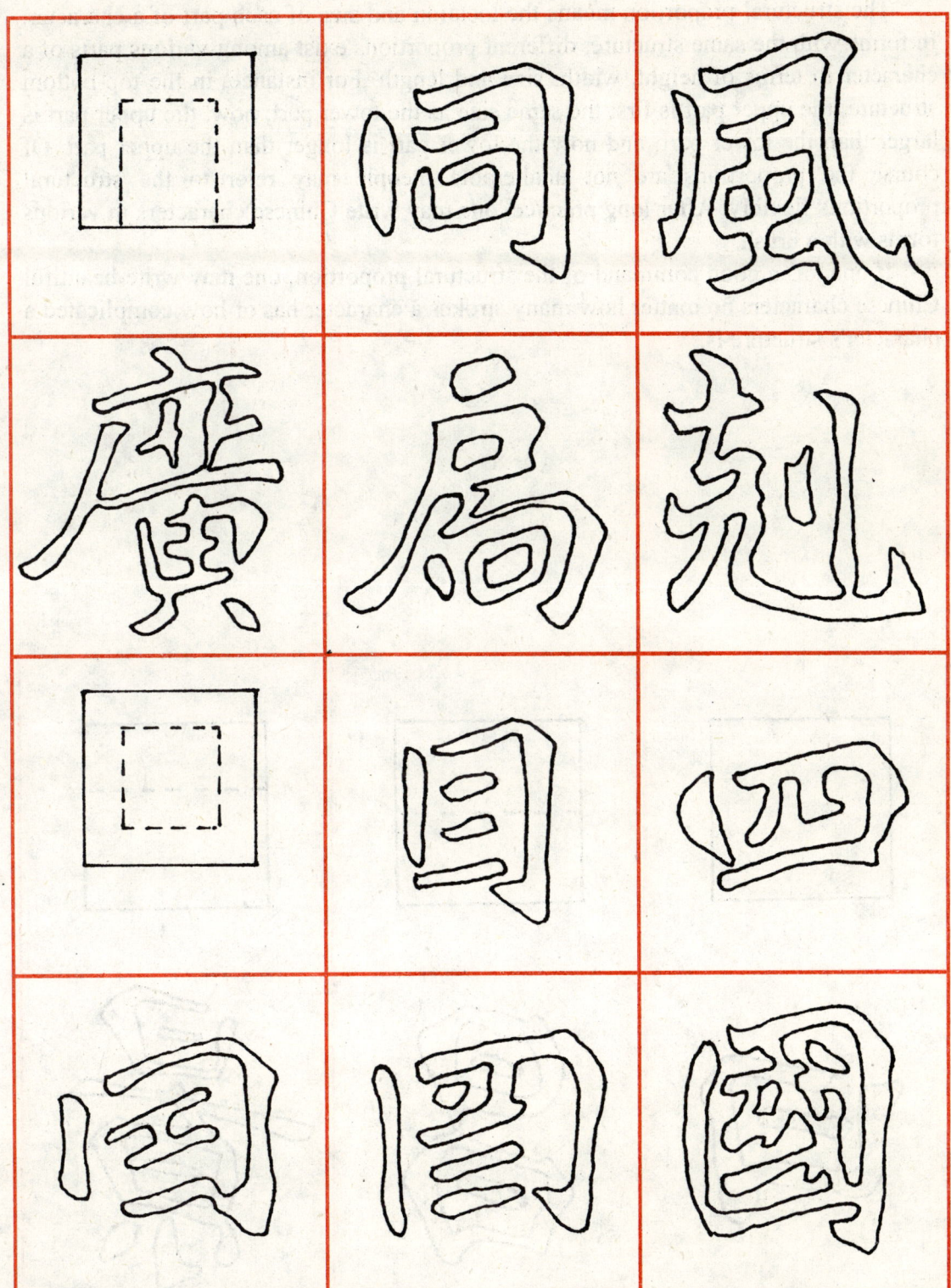

## 2. Structural Proportion

The structural proportion means the location and size of each part of a character. In forms with the same structure, different proportions exist among various parts of a character in terms of height, width, size and length. For instance, in the top-bottom structure, the upper part is first the same size as the lower part; now, the upper part is larger than the lower part; and now the lower part is longer than the upper part. Of course the proportions are not unalterable. People may refer to the structural proportions flexibly. After long practice, one may write Chinese characters in various forms with a brush.

If one has a good command of the structural proportion, one may write beautiful Chinese characters no matter how many strokes a character has or how complicated a character's structure is.

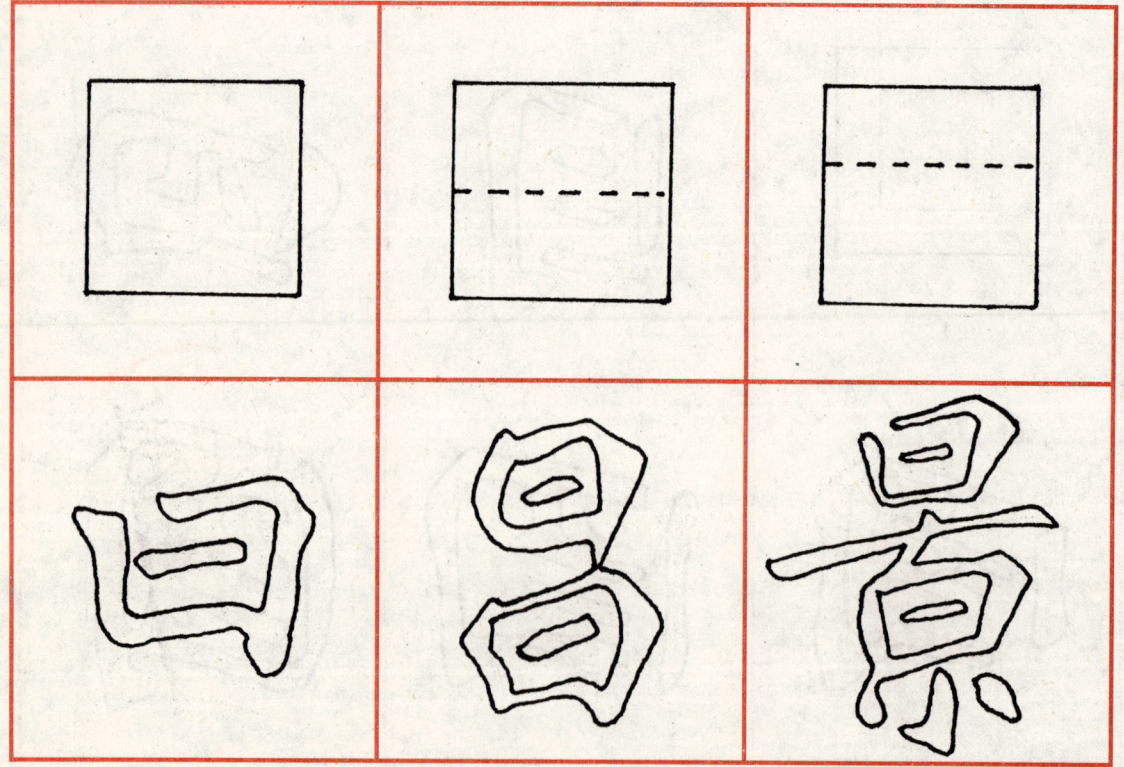

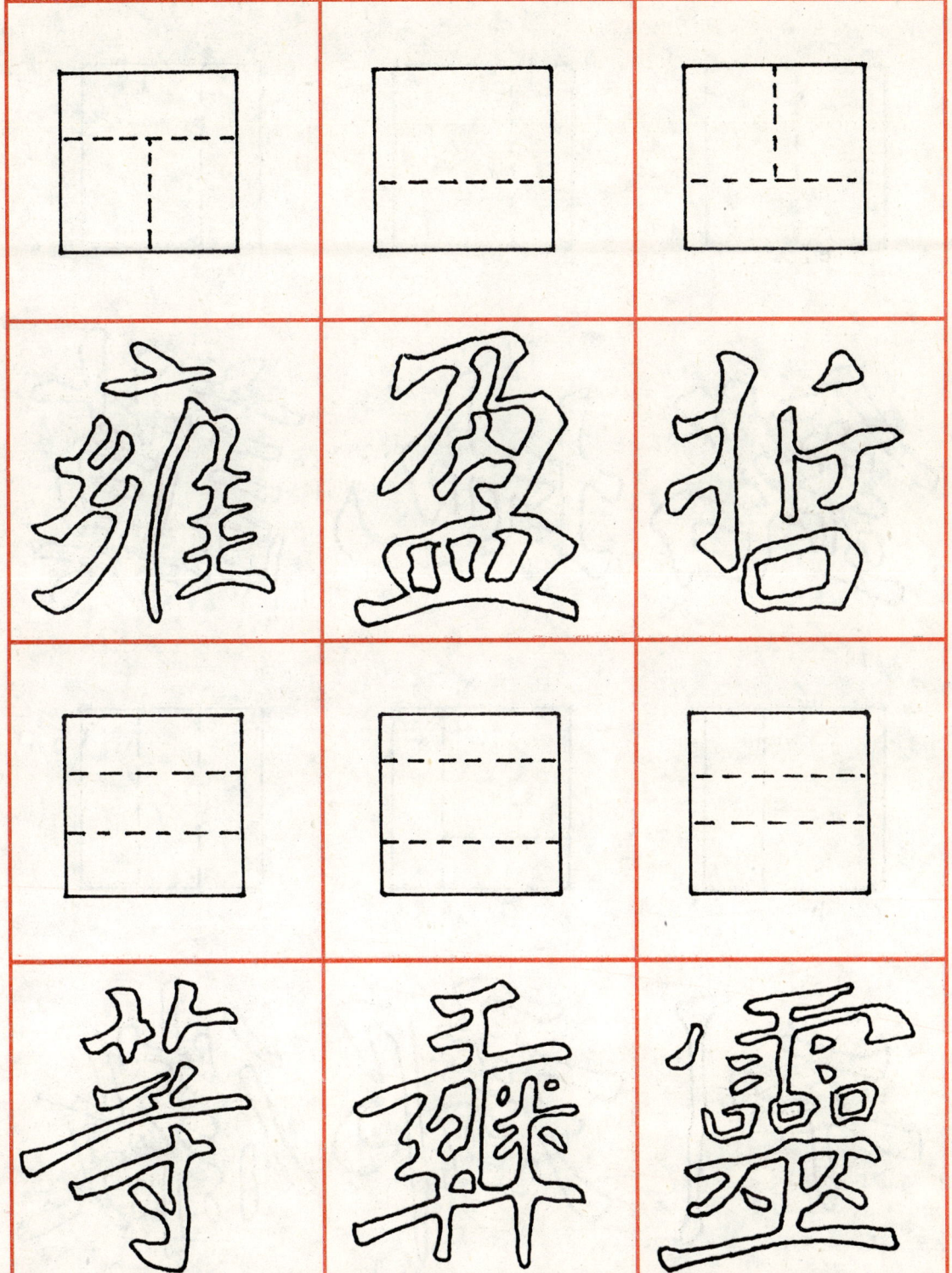

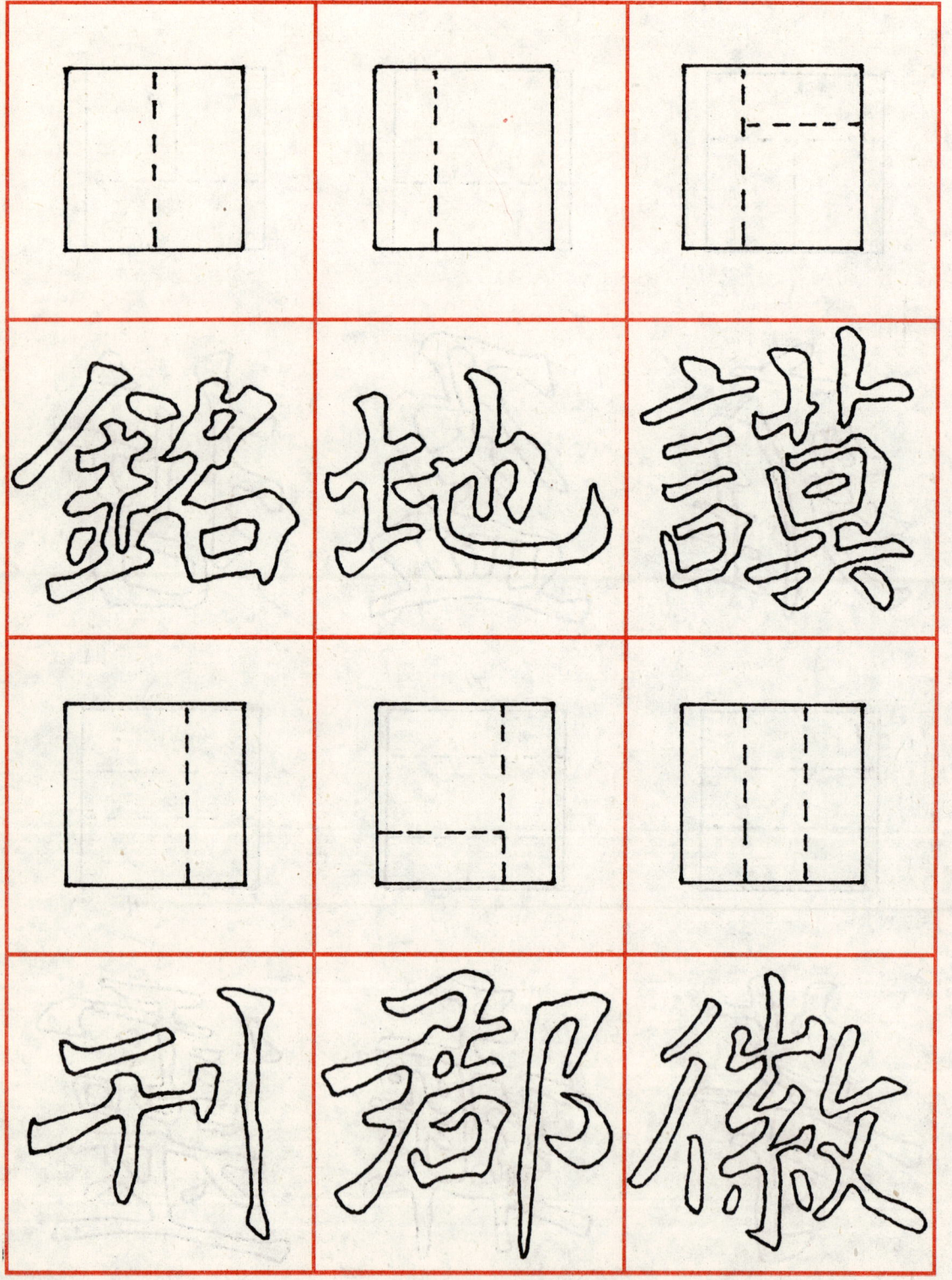

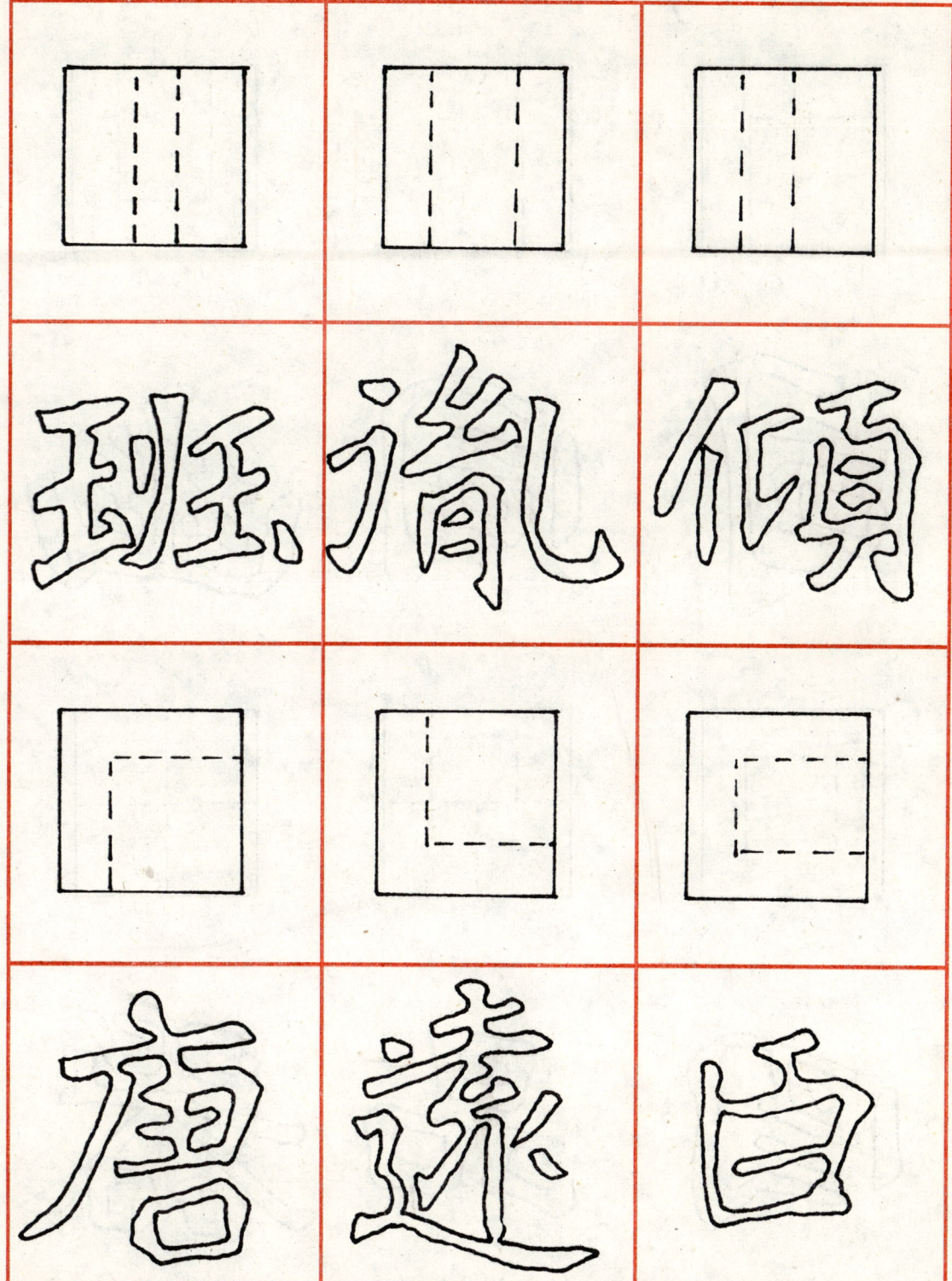

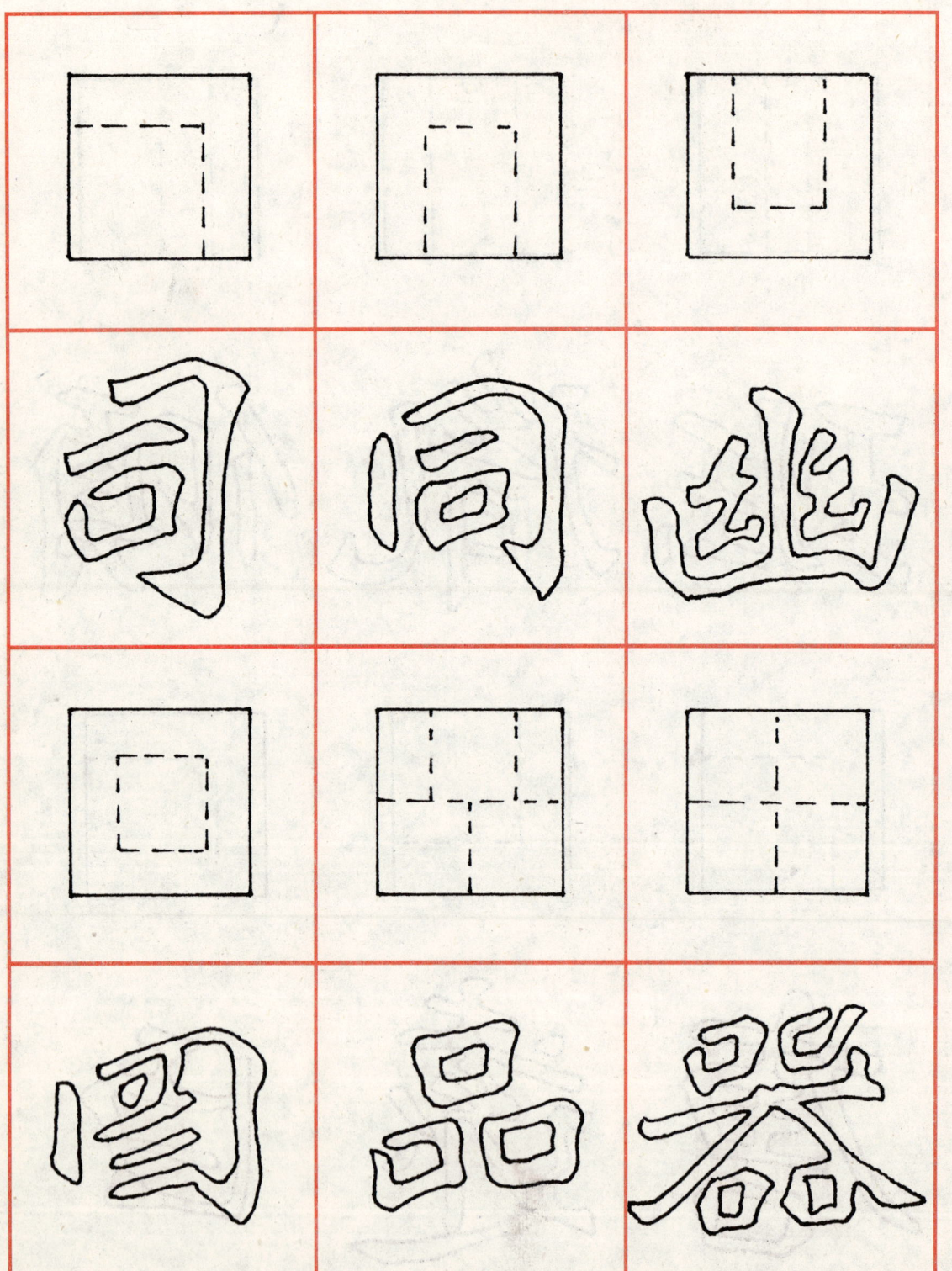

# 3. The Laws of the Structure

The laws of the structure mean the conditions one must have, and the principles one must follow, in creating beautifully shaped Chinese characters.

To understand and master the laws of the structure is very important to the study of the structure. One should not only know how the structure of a character is arranged, but also understand why the character is arranged in such a way. In this way one may better master the rules of the structure and cultivate one's ability to create one's own structures.

Though Wei stone inscriptions do not have strict laws as regular script of the Tang Dynasty, calligraphers must follow some laws and rules. In this way calligraphers can write as they wish but they will not violate the laws of the structure.

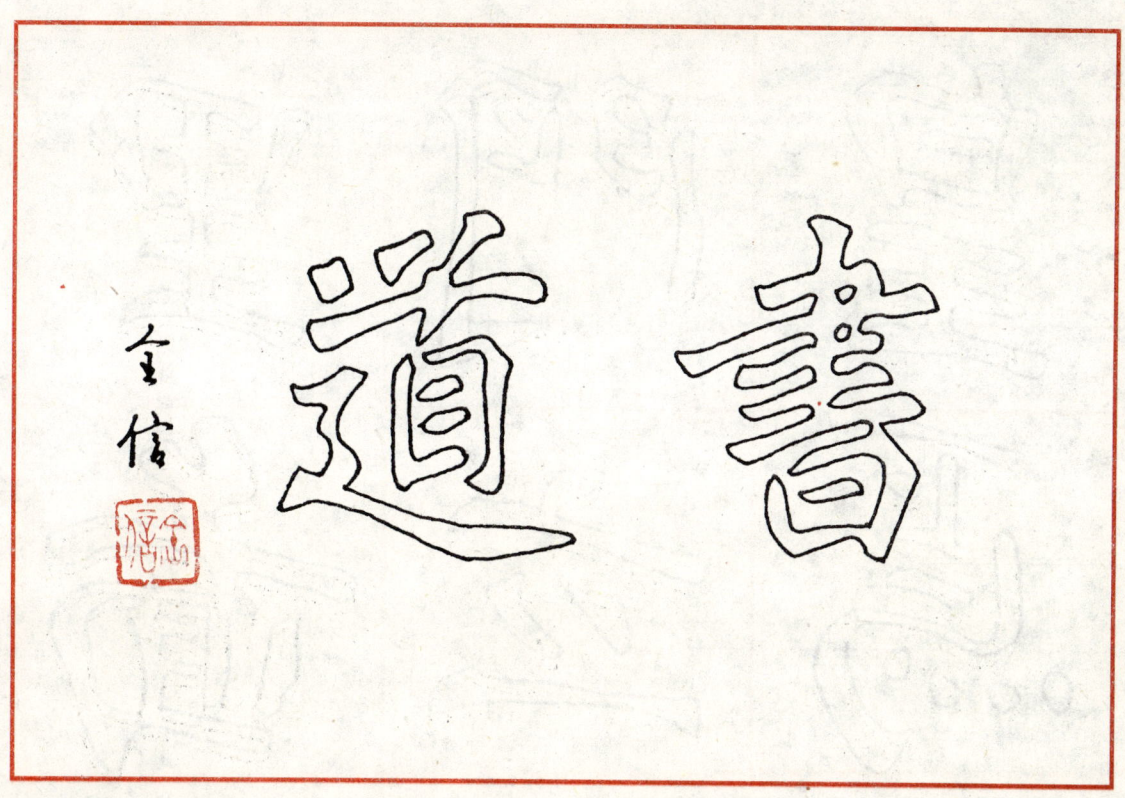

Stability and balance

# Evenness

Strokes should be spaced neither too close nor too far apart.

孝　咸

西　往　紐

無　事　皮

箭　威　磬

# Appropriate Proportions

| | | |
|---|---|---|
| Appropriate proportions between simple and complex strokes and components | 縈 | 稟 |
| 紹 | 茉 | 彙 |
| 季 | 肆 | 緋 |
| 亮 | 稼 | 際 |

# Coherence

Dots and strokes echoing each other

必 正

帝 内 以

父 尤 在

者 哲 豫

Strokes should be drawn out gracefully, each different from the next.

眾 舉

熙 賢 豐

麿 好 龜

縻 撫 擾

# Coordination and Unification

| | | |
|---|---|---|
| Coordinated strokes and a unified style | 賁 | 文 |
| 興 | 民 | 允 |
| 老 | 產 | 光 |
| 我 | 是 | 替 |

# 4. The Layout of the Structure

The layout of the structure refers to the distribution and form of dots and strokes in a block-style character. In a small block, calligraphers may create various shapes of Chinese characters. The layout of the structure must change according to the laws of the structure.

As to a character with short horizontal strokes and long vertical strokes, a vertical form should be taken to write a narrow and long character; as to one with long horizontal strokes and short vertical strokes, a horizontal form should be adopted to produce a broad and short character; as to a character with strokes on all sides, a square character should be written; as to a slanting character, the calligrapher should try to make it well-centered and balanced; as to a single and small character, the calligrapher should make it look large; and as to an overlapped character, the calligrapher should make efforts to create a balanced one.

With regard to the distribution of each part, there are the top-and-bottom, high-and-low, long-and-short, wide-and-narrow, open-and-close, stretching-and-shrinking relations.

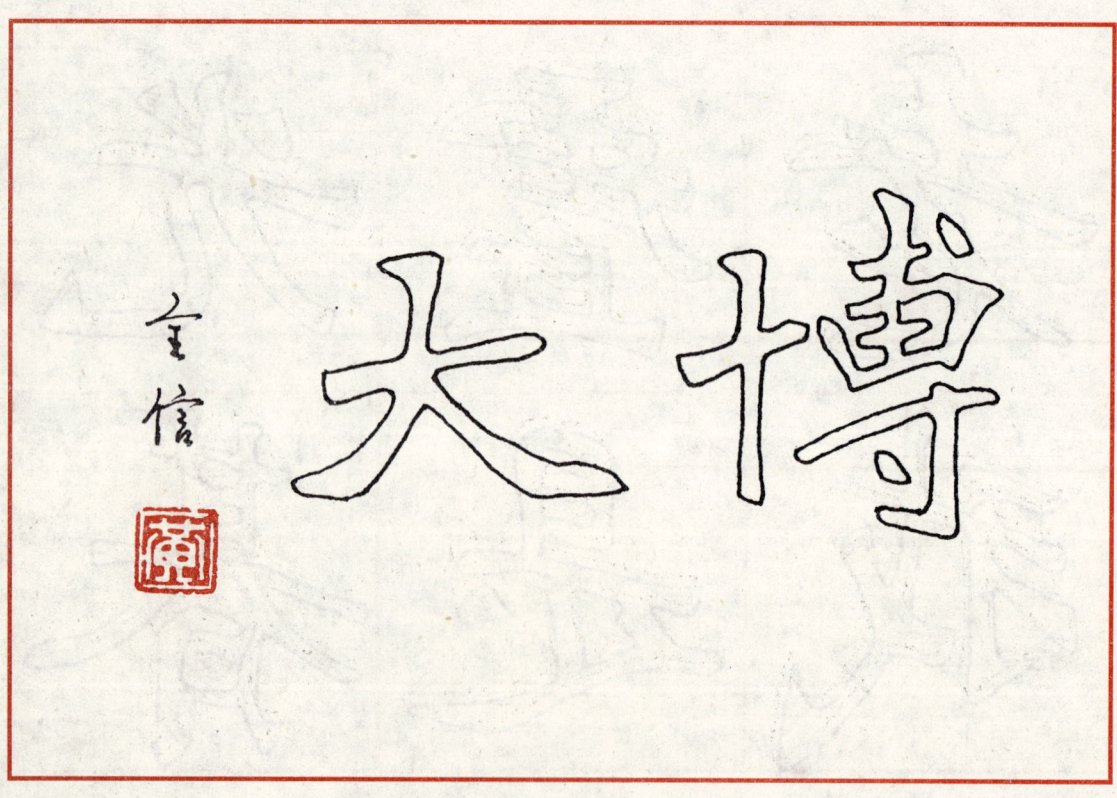

# Top and Bottom

| | | |
|---|---|---|
| To level the top of a character with a small left part | 氓 | 壇 |
| To level the bottom if a character has a small right part. | 散 | 勃 |
| A flat-top character should have a leveled head. | 拜 | 郎 |
| A flat-bottom character should have leveled feet. | 諸 | 鏈 |

# High and Low

| | | |
|---|---|---|
| As to left-dominant characters, the left is higher than the right. | 斯 | 都 |
| As to right-dominant characters, the left is low and the right high. | 波 | 博 |
| As to a character with two same parts, the left is low and the right, high. | 羽 | 朤 |
| As to the left-center-right characters, some parts are high and the others low. | 徽 | 懄 |

# Long and Short

| | | |
|---|---|---|
| A short horizontal stroke and a long left-falling stroke | 左 | 右 |
| A long horizontal stroke and a short left-falling stroke | 不 | 方 |
| A long horizontal stroke and a short vertical stroke | 十 | 早 |
| A short horizontal stroke and a long vertical stroke | 中 | 年 |

| | | |
|---|---|---|
| As to "roofed-in" characters, the top is wide, and the bottom, narrow. | 金 | 登 |
| As to "floored-in" characters, the "floor" is wider than the top. | 暨 | 盤 |
| As to characters with the top as the mainstay, the top is wide and the bottom, narrow. | 耆 | 勲 |
| As to characters with the bottom playing the leading role, the bottom is wide and the top, narrow. | 舻 | 巍 |

# Open and Close

| | | |
|---|---|---|
| As to a character with a short horizontal stroke and a long vertical stroke, the left-falling and the right-falling strokes should move apart. | 未 | 東 |
| As to a character with a long horizontal stroke and a short vertical stroke, the left-falling stroke should end up closer to the right-falling one. | 梁 | 深 |
| As to a character with some left-falling and right-falling strokes, some are far away and the others are close to each other. | 寮 | 慕 |
| The upper should be open, and the down angle, be closed. | 雨 | 尚 |

# Stretching and Shrinking

As to a character with a left-falling stroke and a right vertical one, the left should shrink and the right stretch.

As to a character with a left vertical stroke and a right-falling stroke, the left should shrink and the right stretch.

As to a character with vertical strokes on both the left and right, the left should shrink and the right stretch.

As to a character with a hooking and a rising stroke, the hooking should shrink and the rising, stretch.

# 5. Outline of the Structure

Chinese characters developed from the irregularly shaped inscriptions on bones or tortoise shells of the Shang Dynasty (c. 16-11th century BC), to later rectangle seal characters, broad square official script and finally square regular script.

Chinese characters have been known as block-style characters. As a matter of fact not all Chinese characters are square ones of the same size. Within a square, many characters have developed into the shapes of the circle, rhombus, triangle, and trapezoid. Even square characters vary in sizes.

To understand the outline of the structure will help us know the structure of a character as a whole.

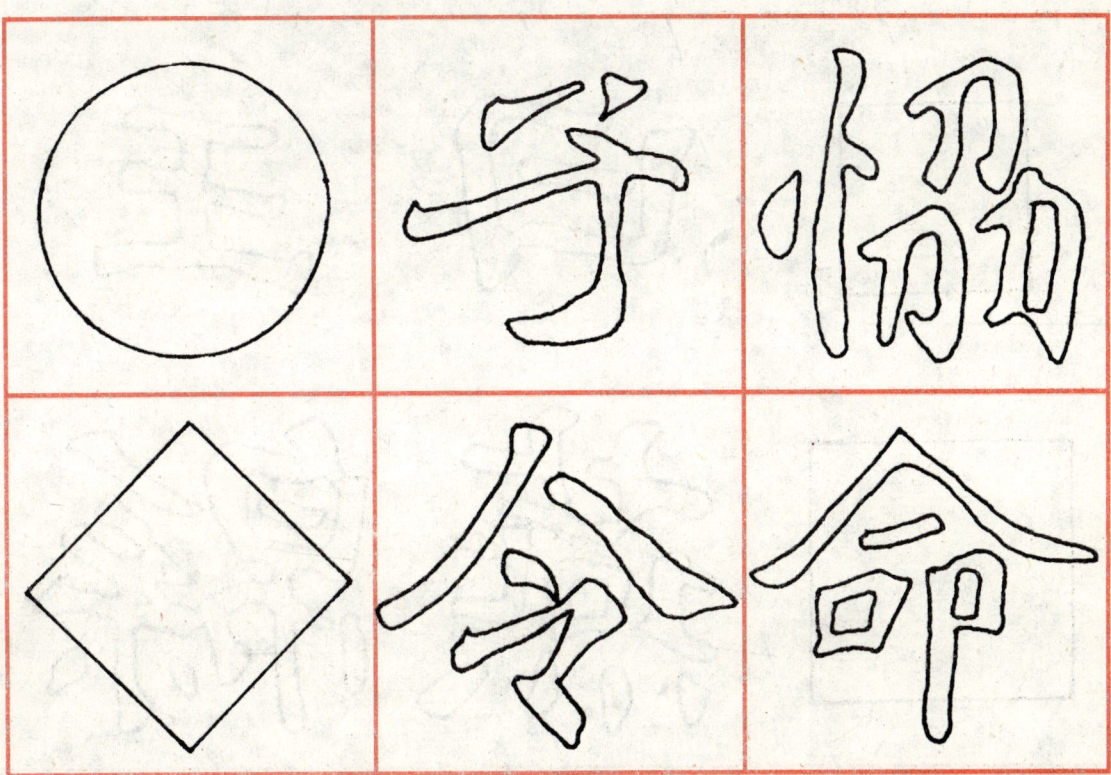

| | | |
|---|---|---|
| □ | 月 | 馬 |
| □ | 四 | 心 |
| □ | 曰 | 王 |
| □ | 燕 | 縣 |

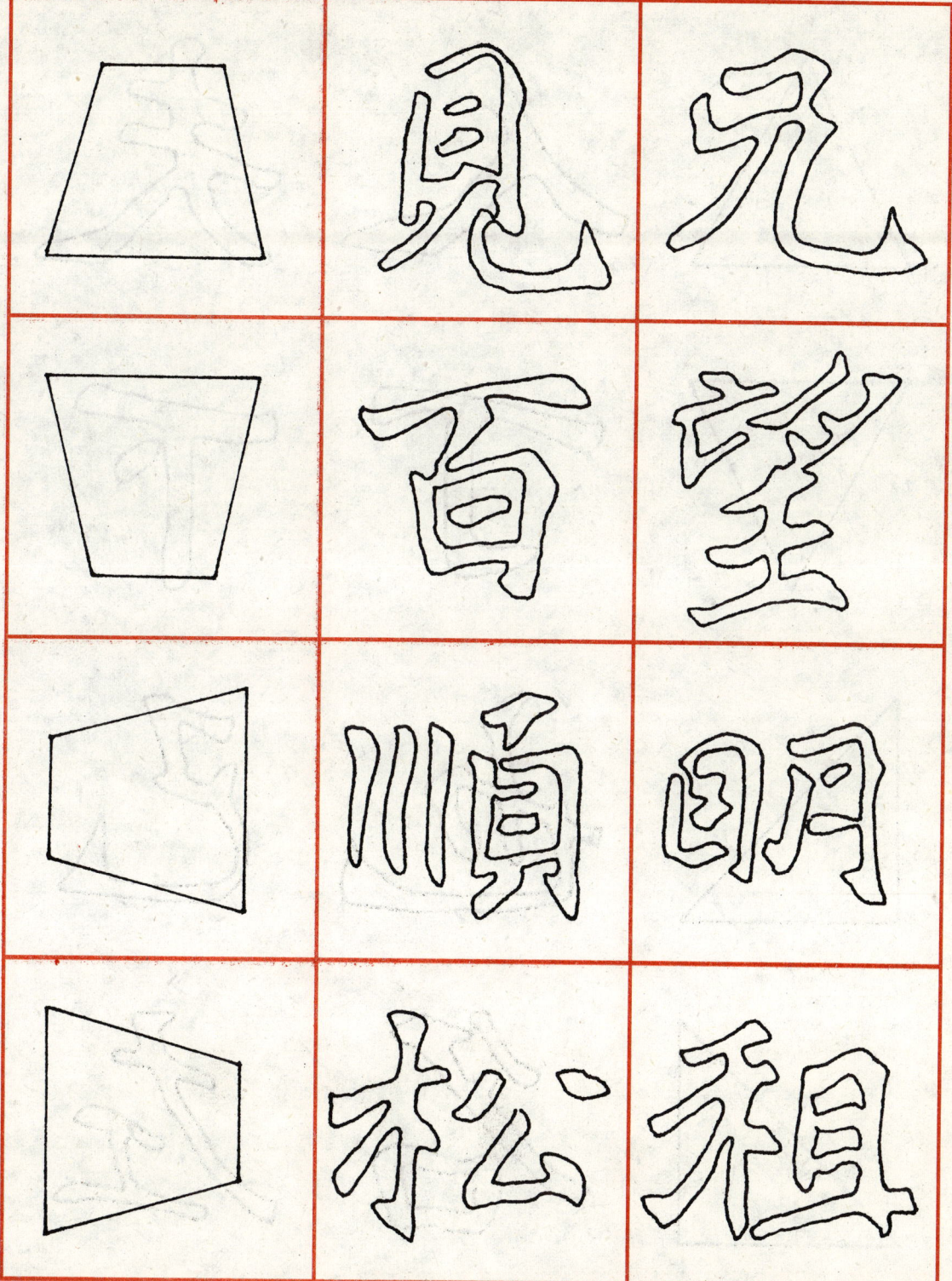

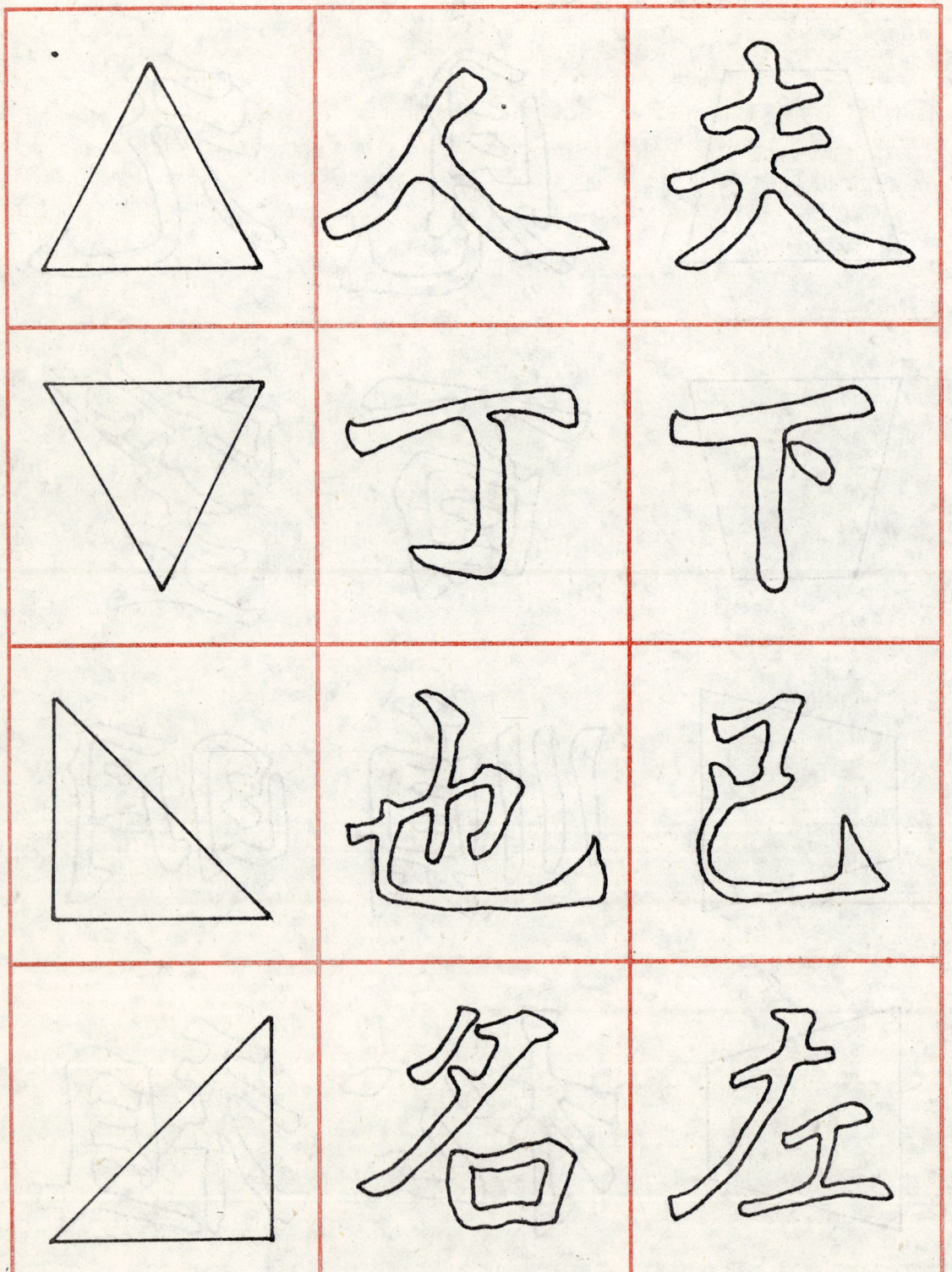

## 6. Changes in the Structure

Among the laws for creating the beauty of Chinese calligraphy, diversification and unification are the most important. Unification depends on echoing and coordination; and diversification, on contrasting changes. Contrast is the most fundamental means, such as square and round, curved and straight, thick and thin, hidden and exposed, light and heavy, gradual and rapid, tough and gentle, dry and wet, etc. Change is one of the important differences between the art of calligraphy and characters written with a writing brush.

Wang Xizhi, a sage of calligraphy, wrote the *Preface to the Orchid Pavilion*, in which a Chinese character 之 appeared more than 20 times, each of them having its own style and shape.

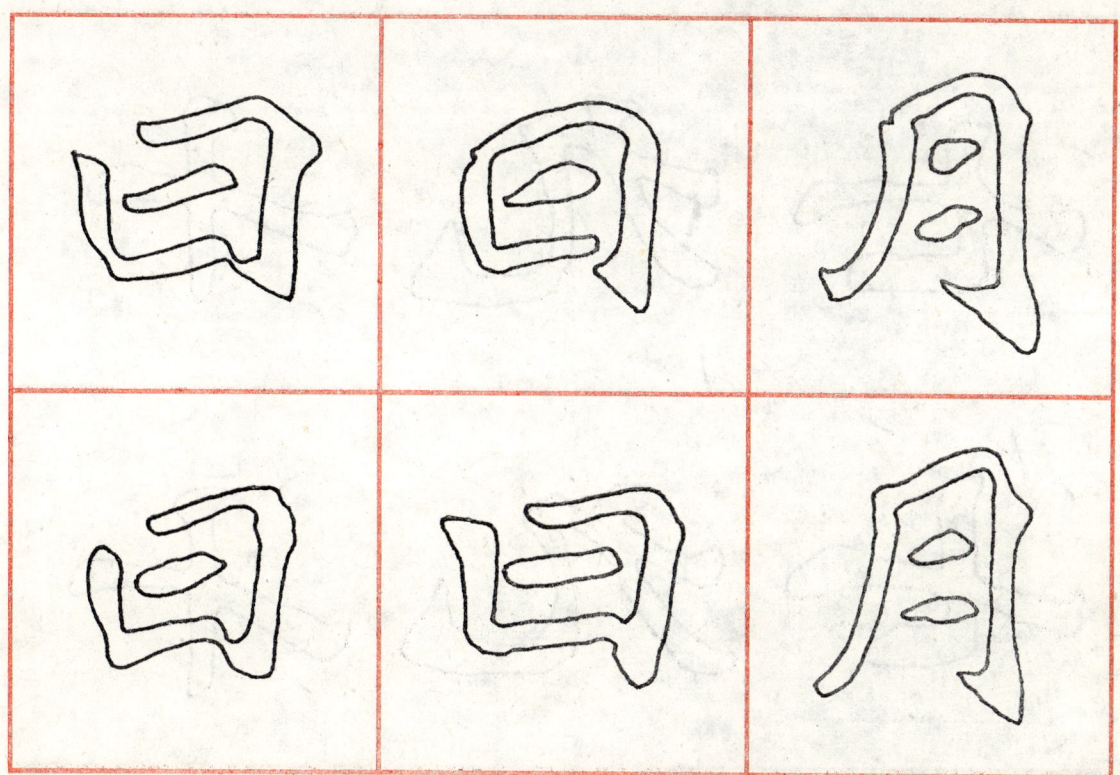

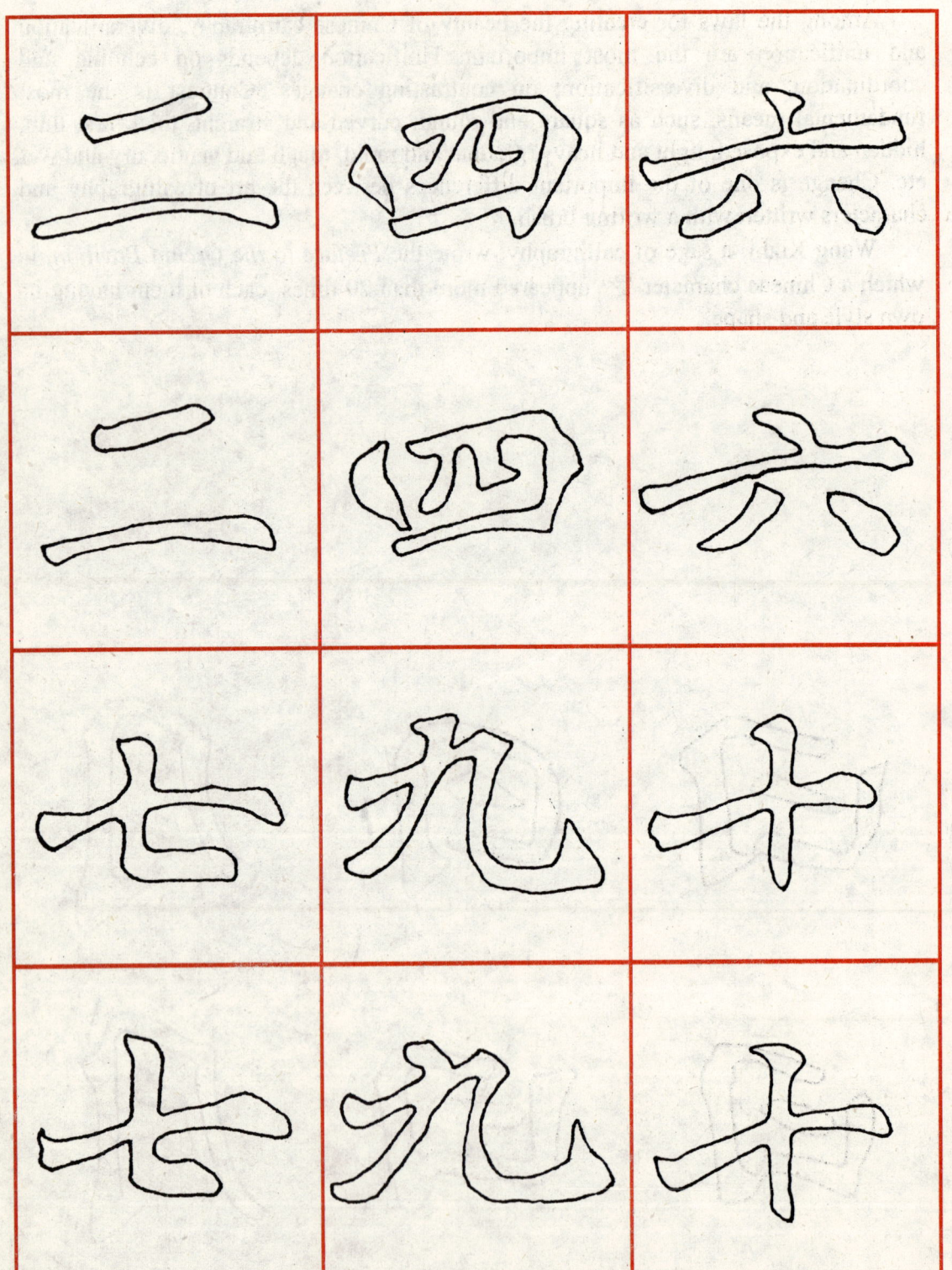

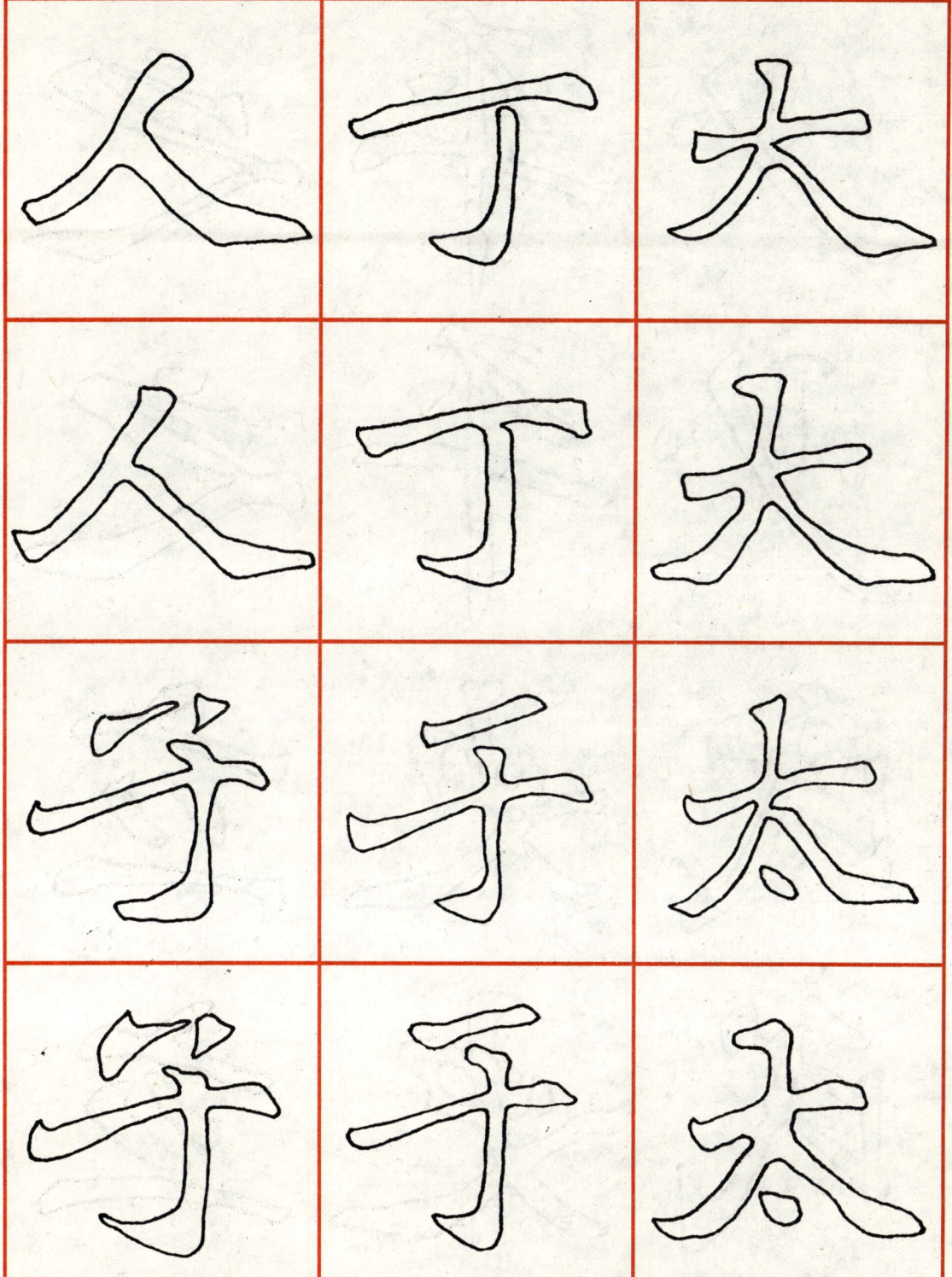

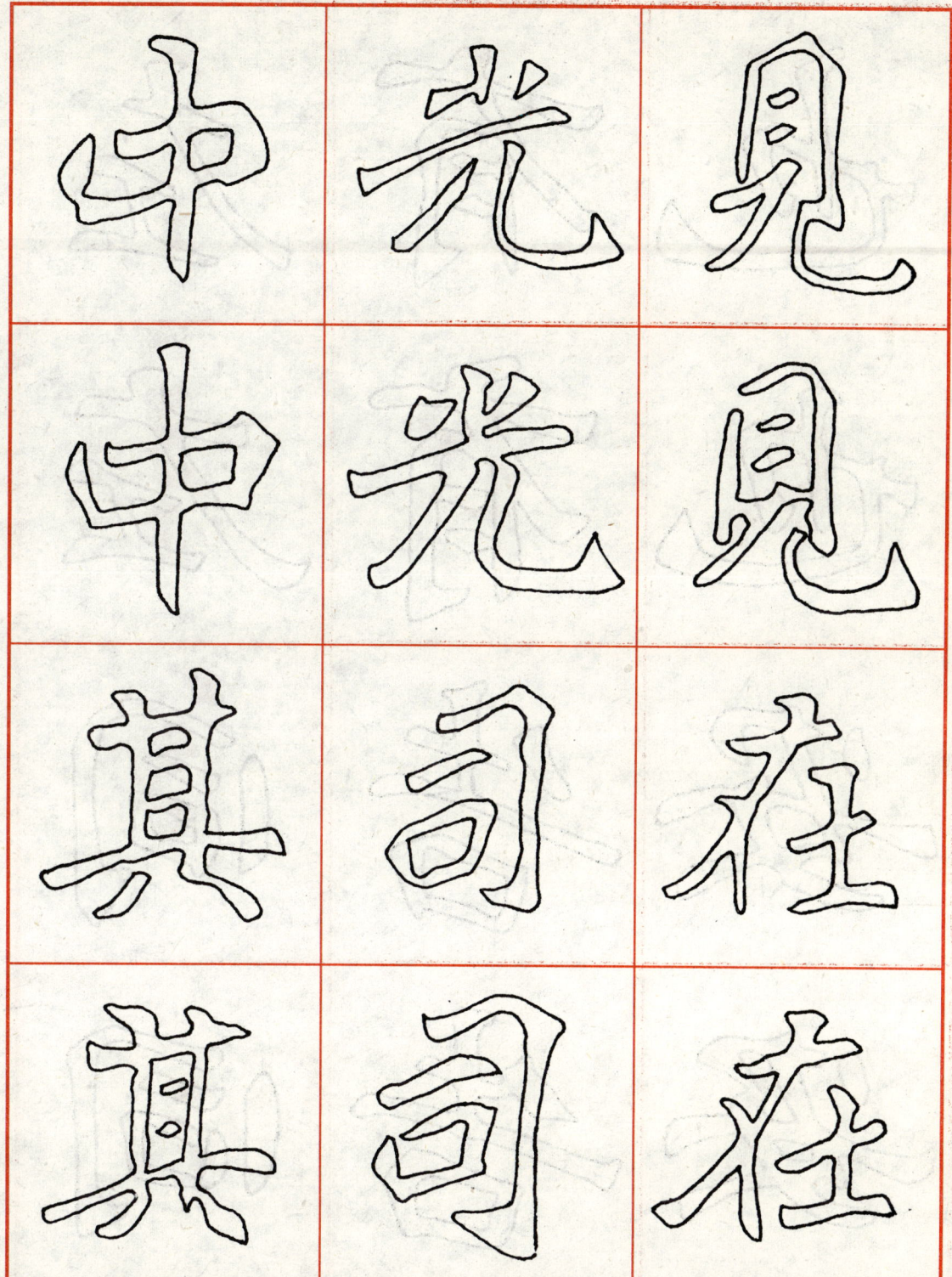

中中其其光光司司見見在在

也 有 左
也 有 左
姿 告 同
姿 告 同

早 寺 軍
早 寺 軍
居 書 事
居 書 事

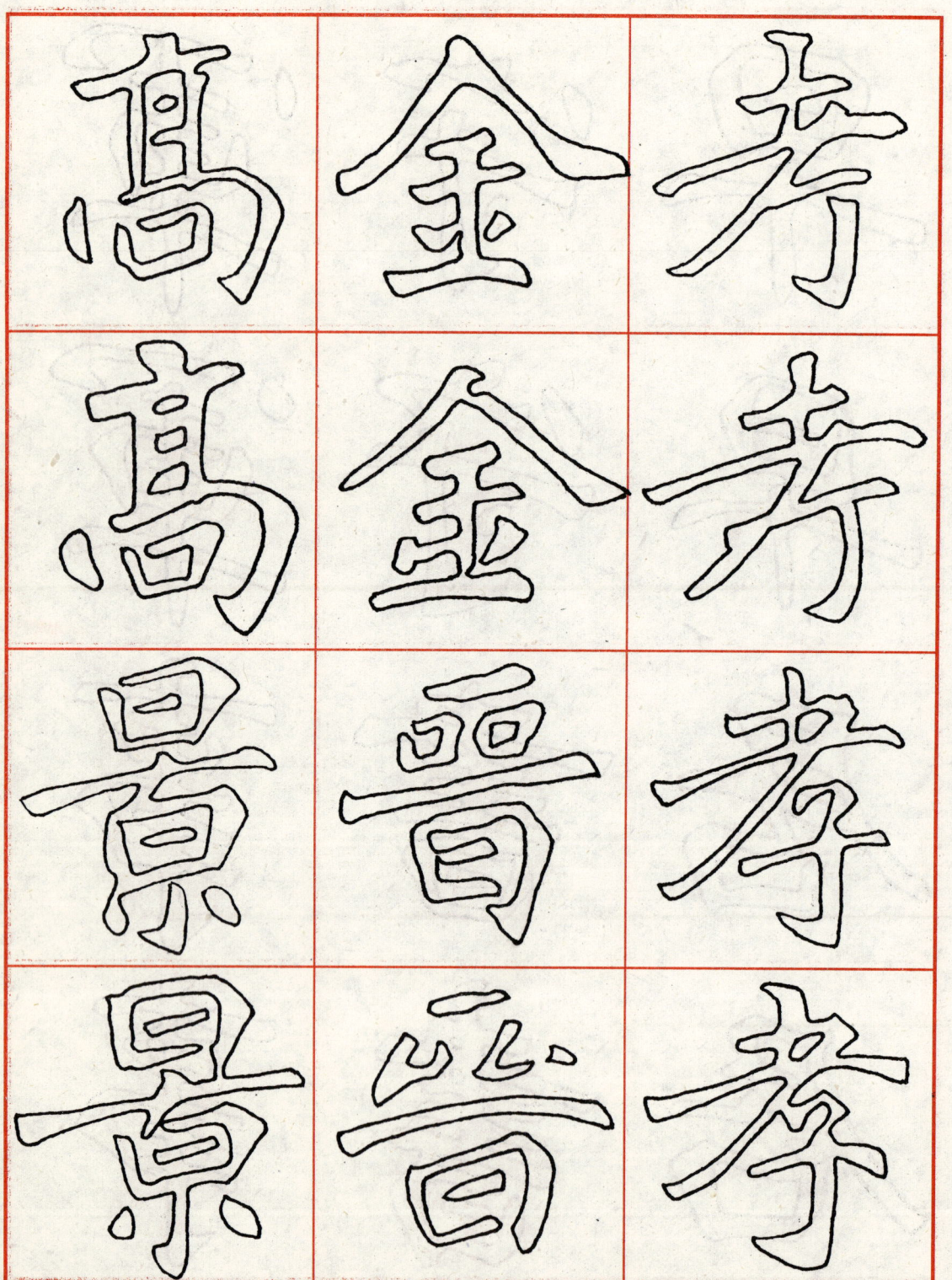

忠 義 妻
忠 義 妻
岳 泉 雍
岳 泉 雍

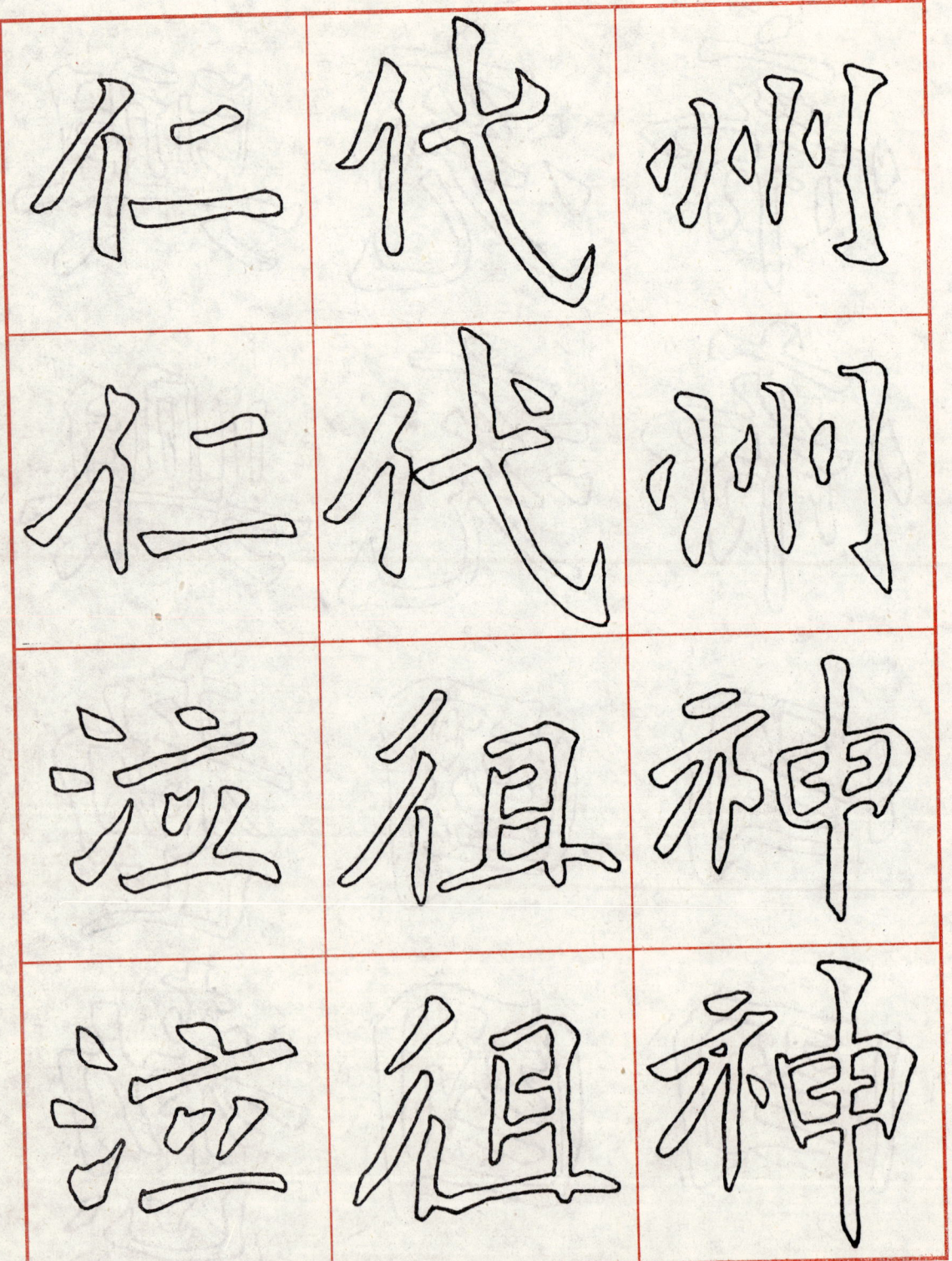

和　將　位
和　將　位
惟　治　侍
惟　治　侍

深 秋 牧

深 秋 牧

洛 郎 使

洛 郎 使

故　德　散
故　德　散
俟　陽　諸
俟　陽　諸

# Chapter VI   Tracing and Copying

Tracing and copying are two different ways to learn Chinese calligraphy. A beginner should start with tracing, and take copying as the mainstay.

Tracing: Place a piece of transparent paper on top of the model and trace it with brush and ink as exactly as possible.

Copying: Put the model in front of the writer and copy characters as accurately as possible.

There are many ways to copy Chinese characters: line copying, check copying, frame copying, contrasting copying, back copying, copying from memory, enlarging copying and shrinking copying.

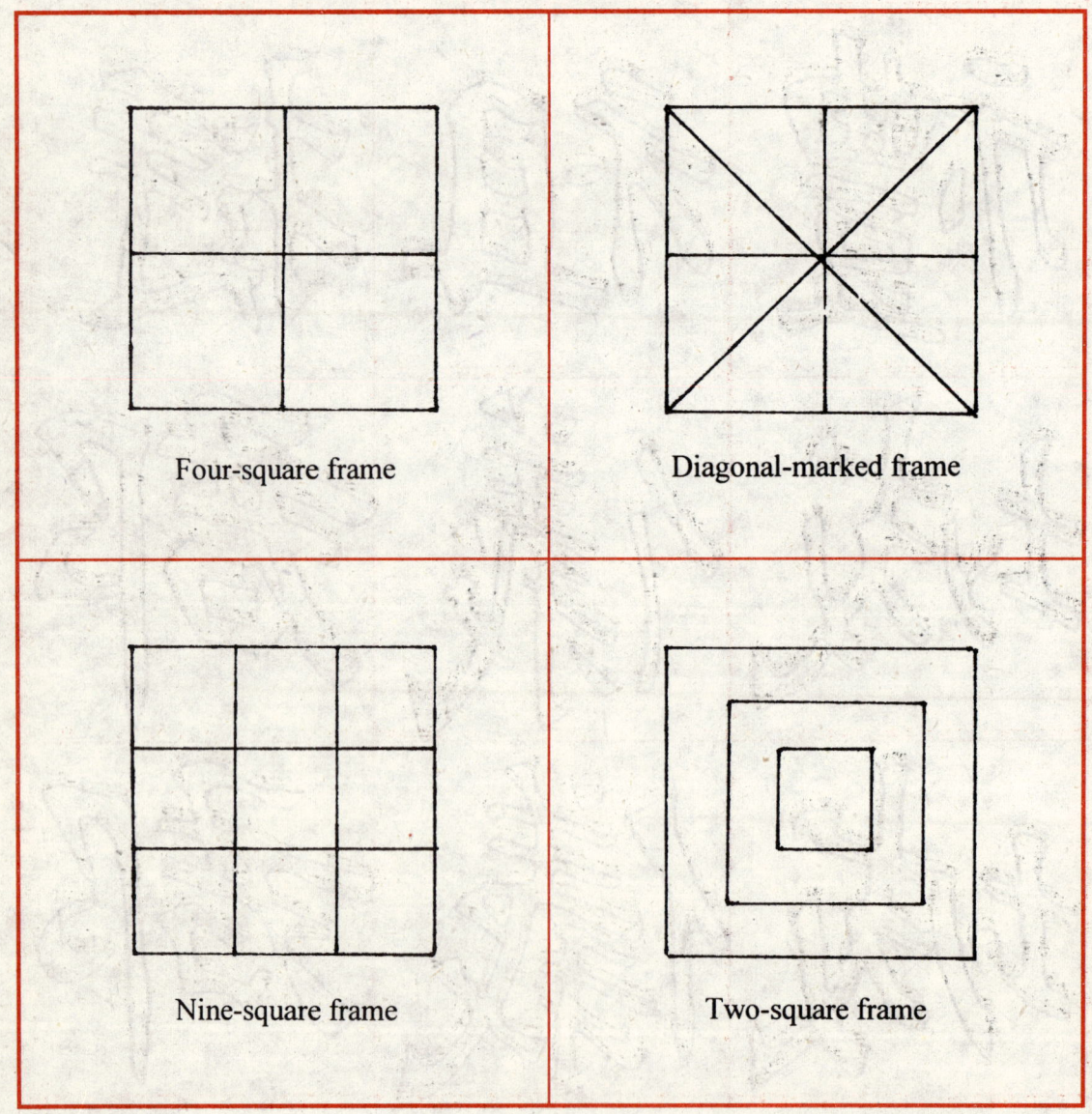

Four-square frame

Diagonal-marked frame

Nine-square frame

Two-square frame

## 1. Four-Square Frame

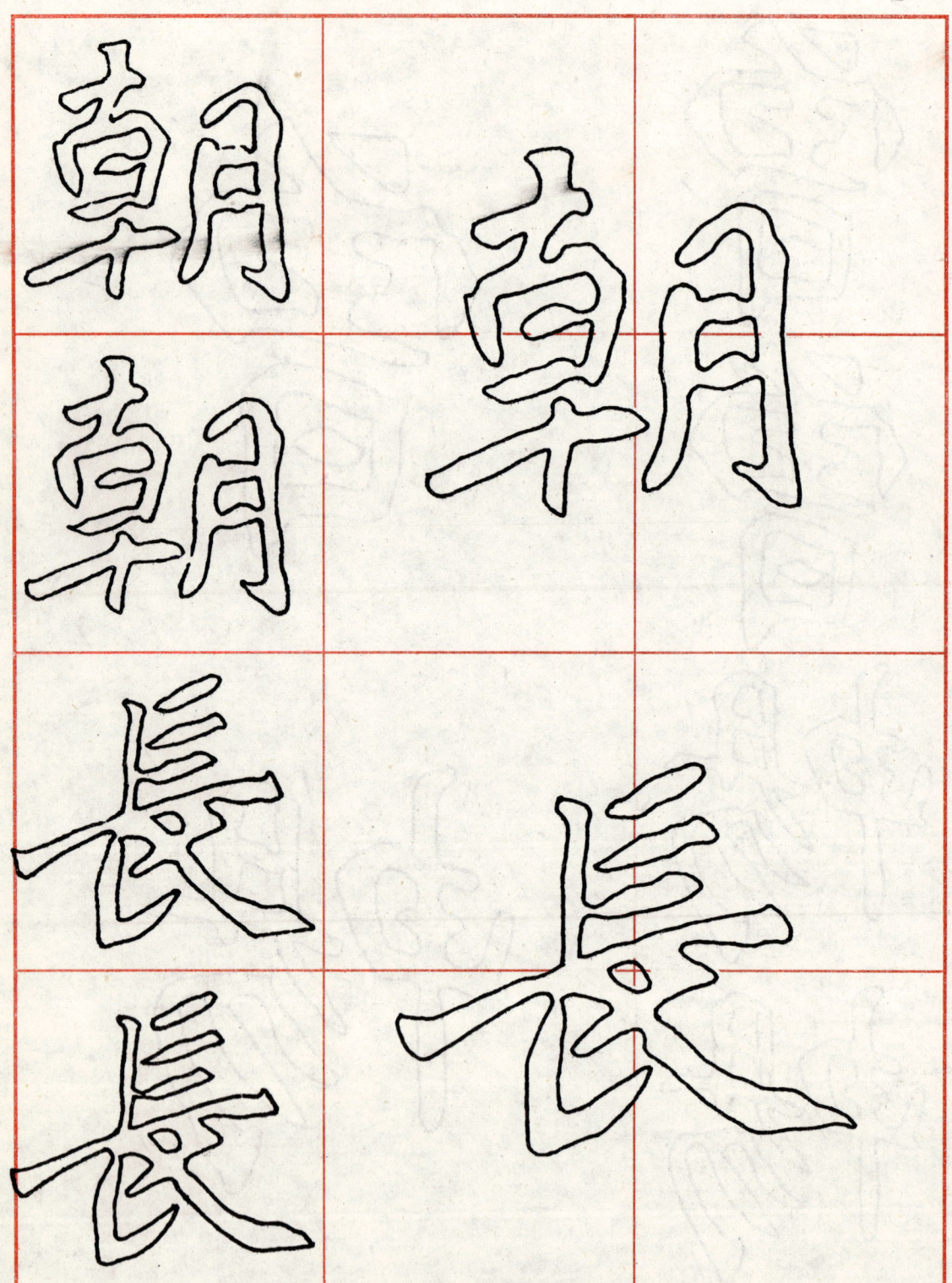

傅
傅
楚
楚

傅
林
延

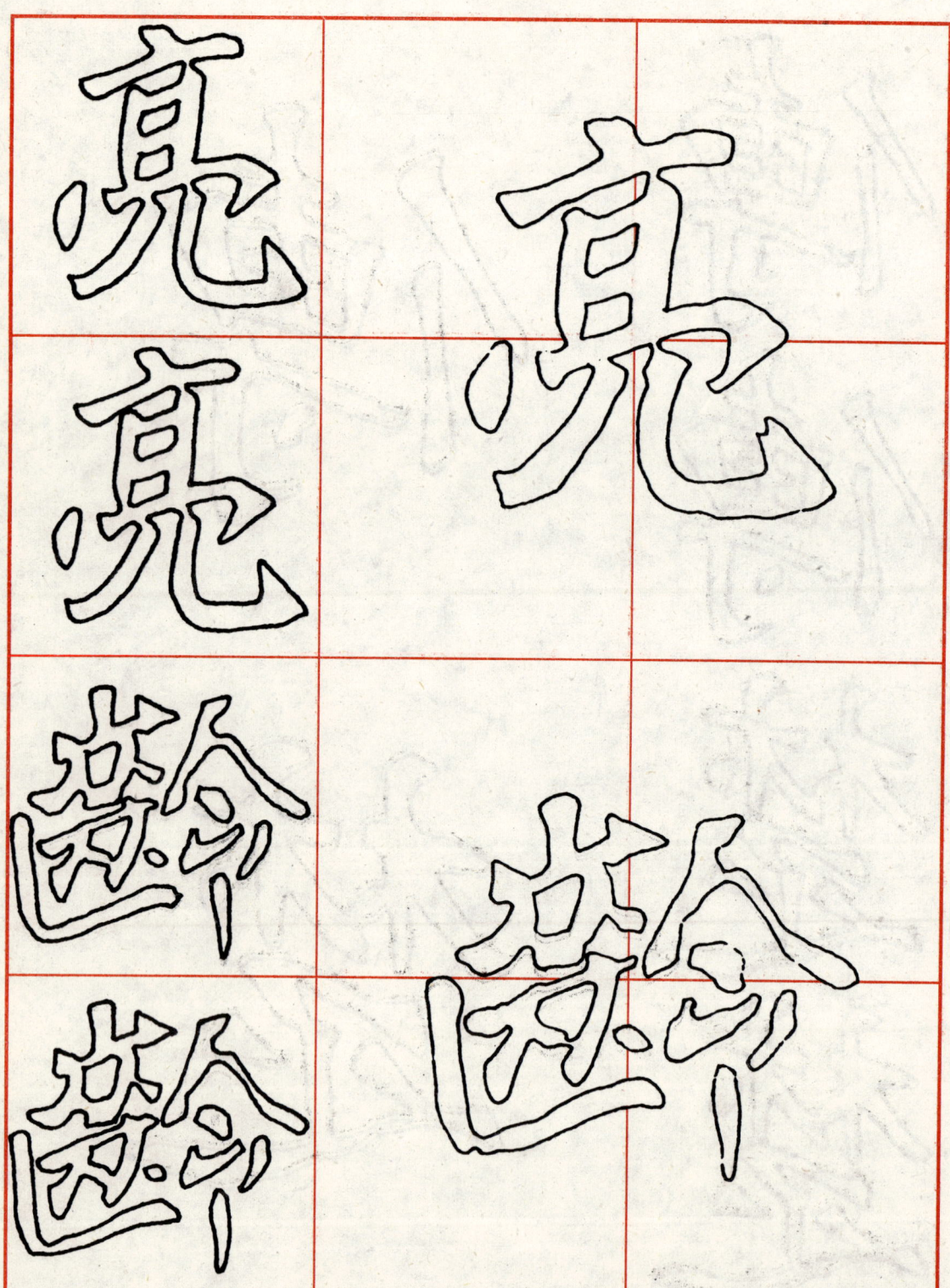

## 2. Diagonal-Marked Frame

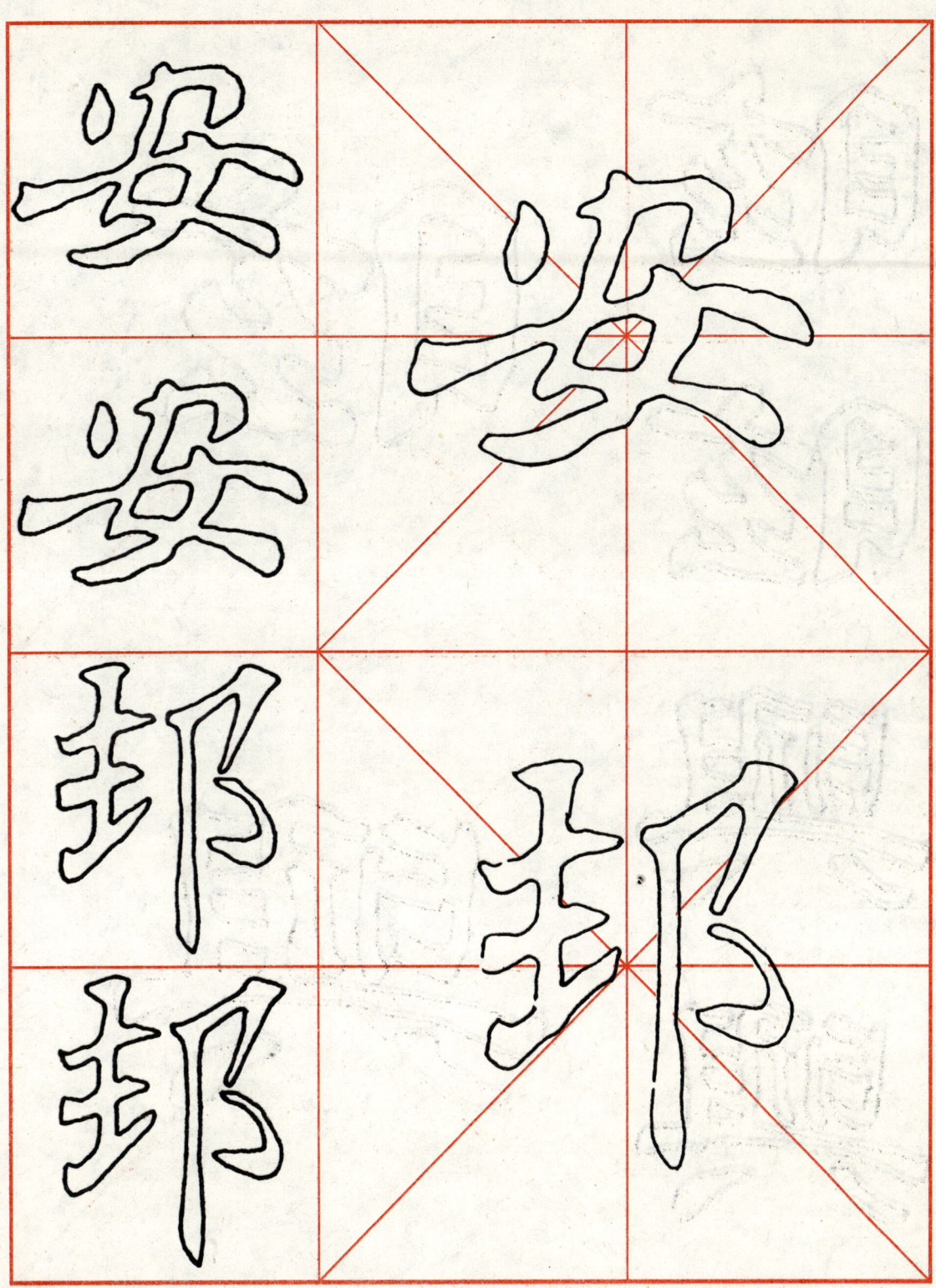

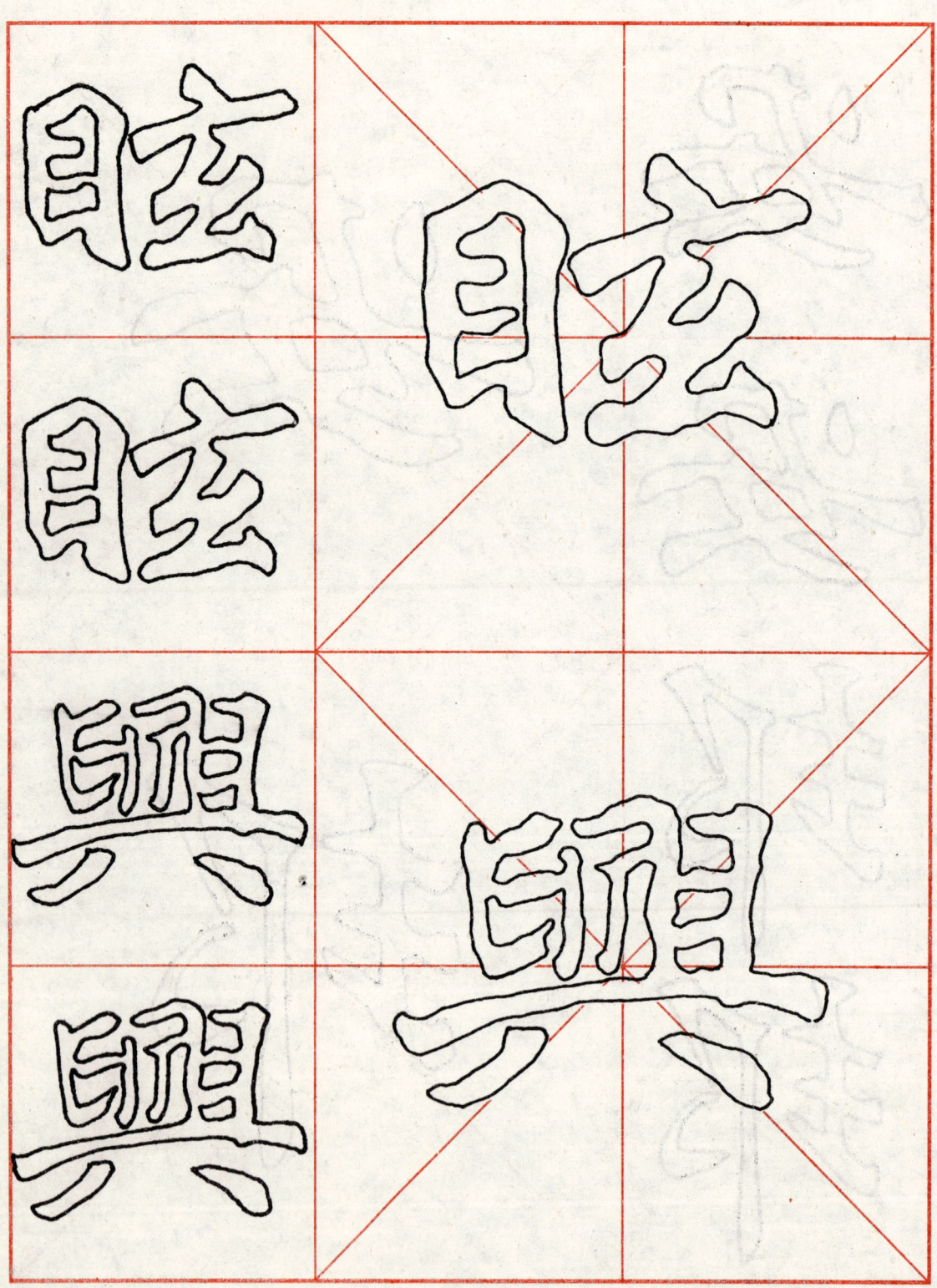

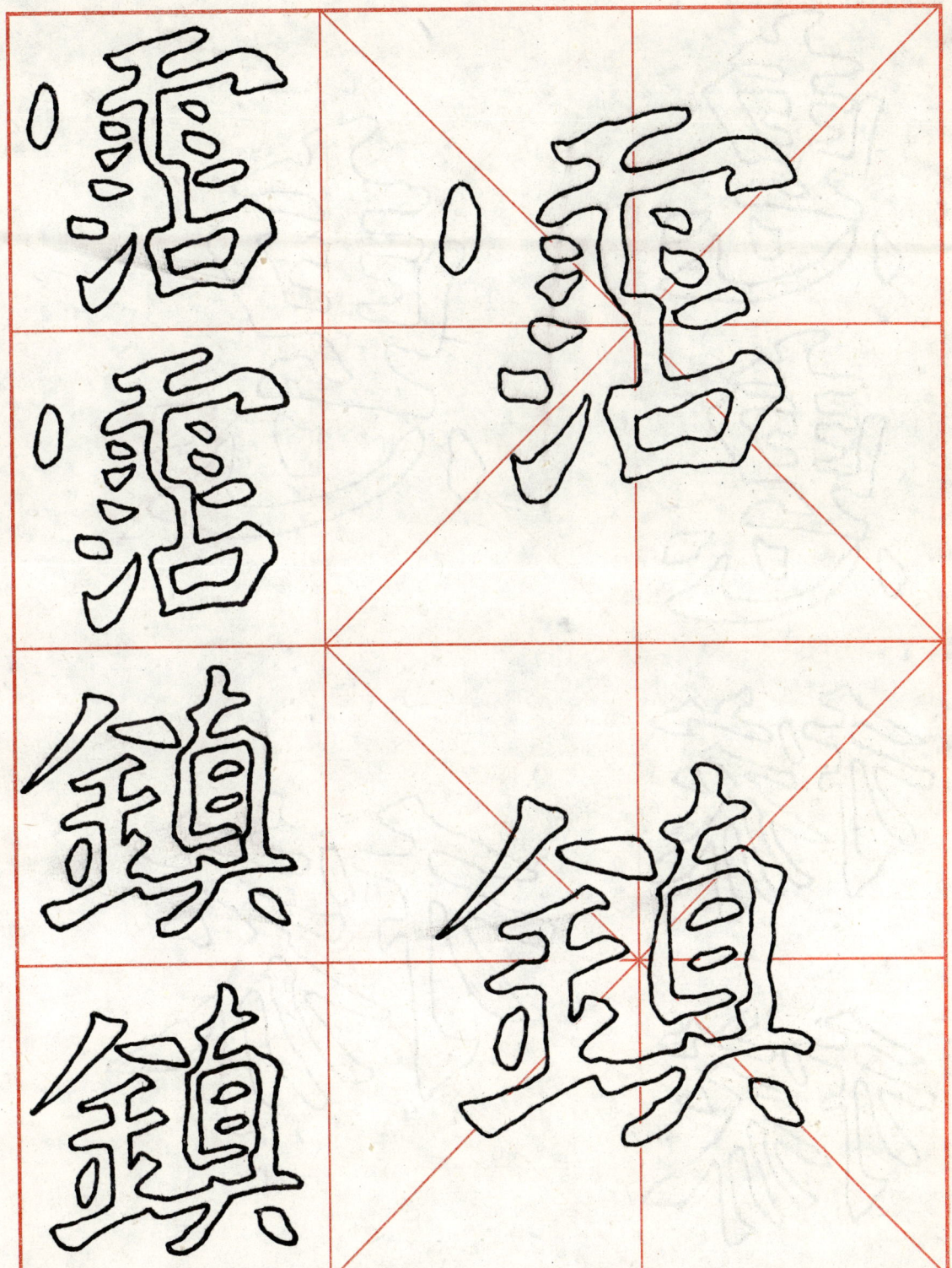

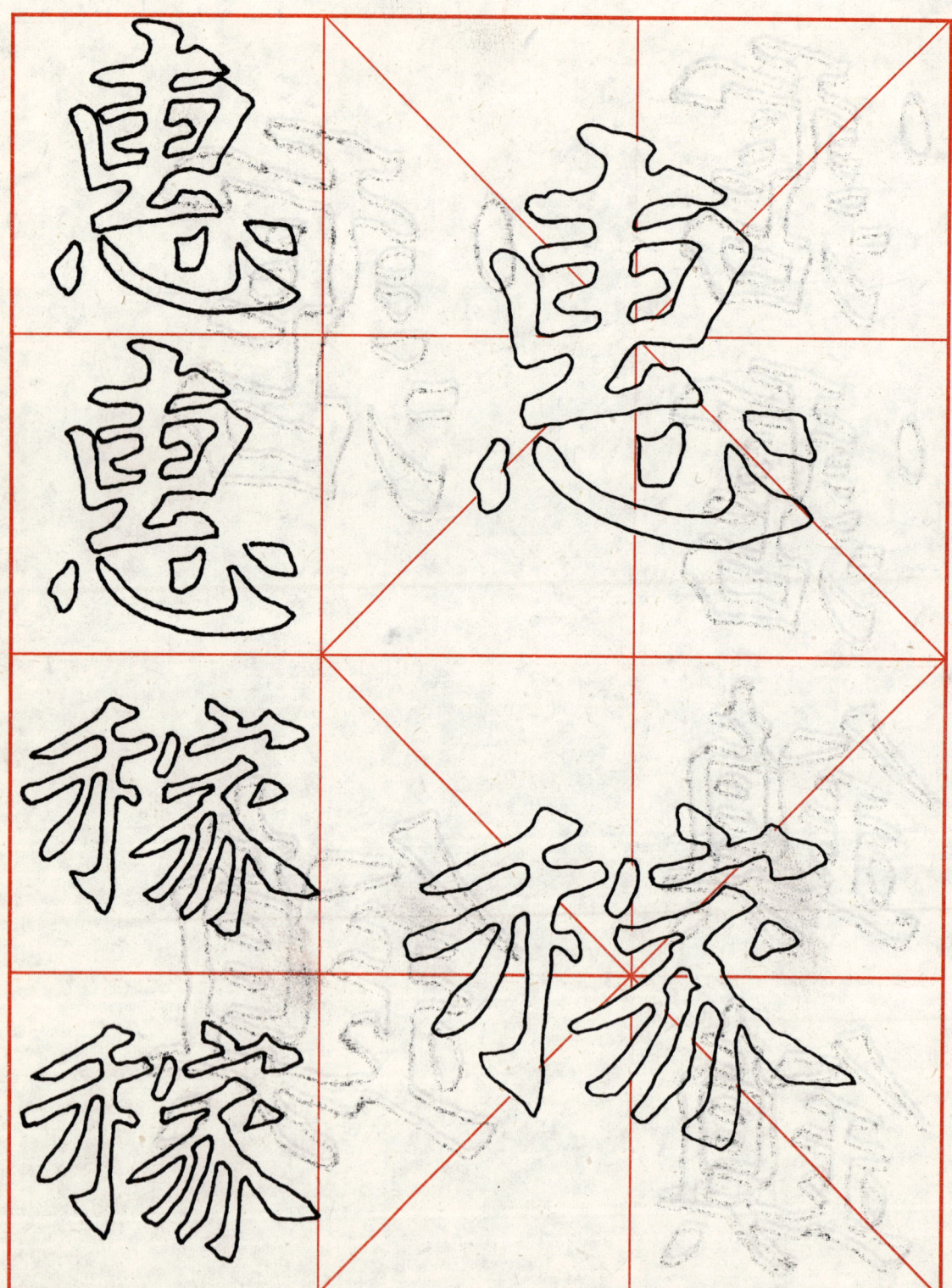

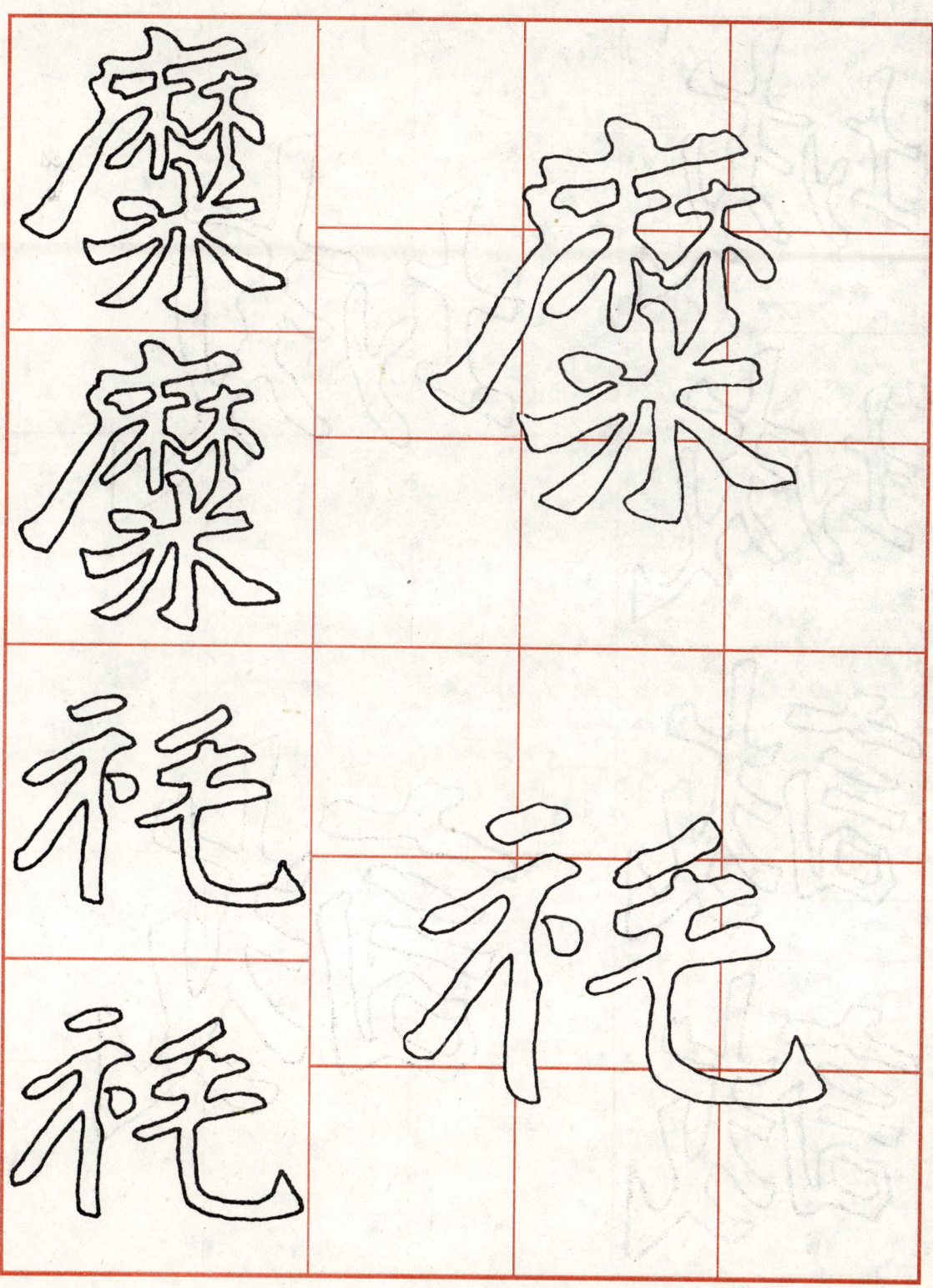

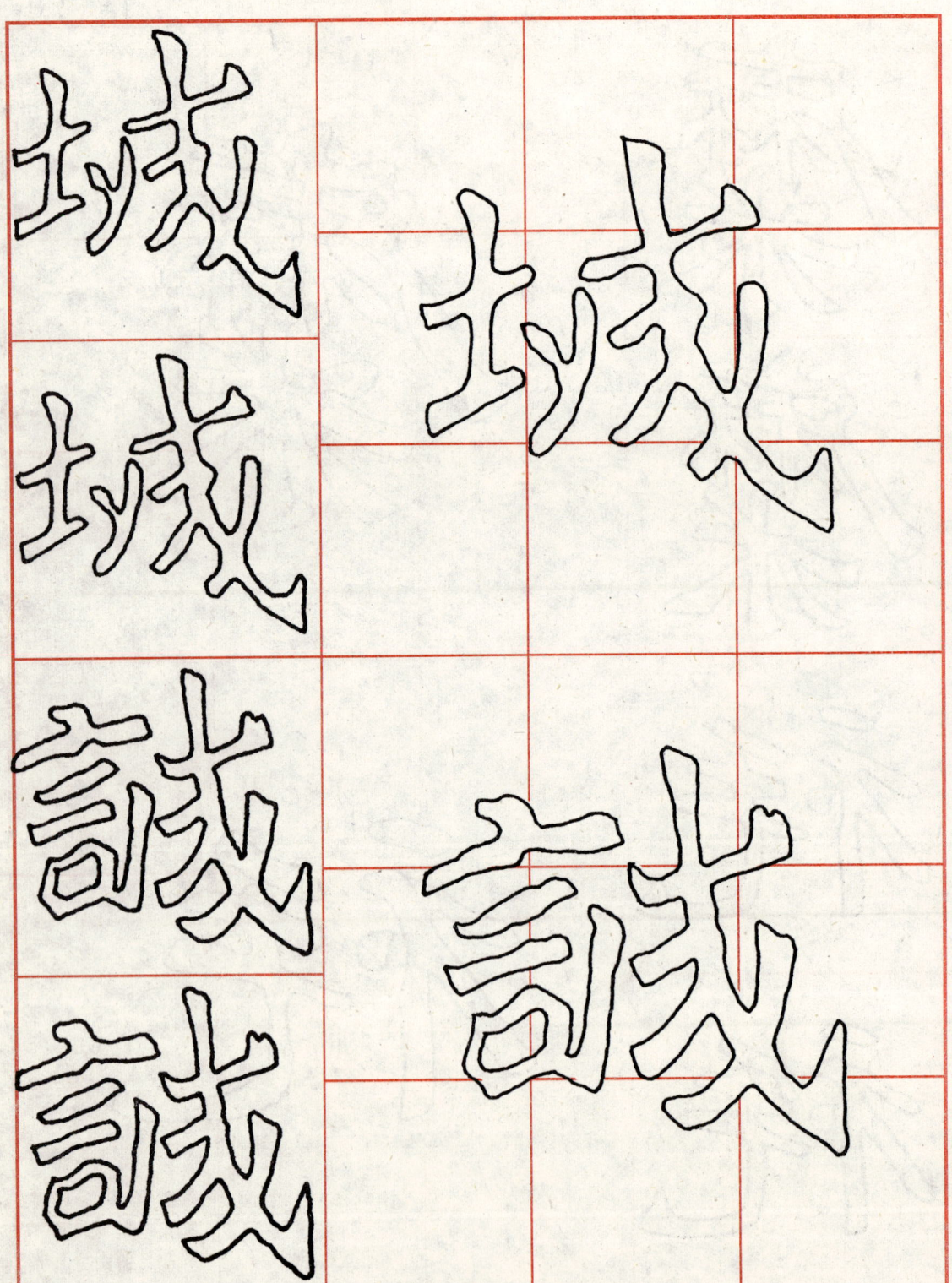

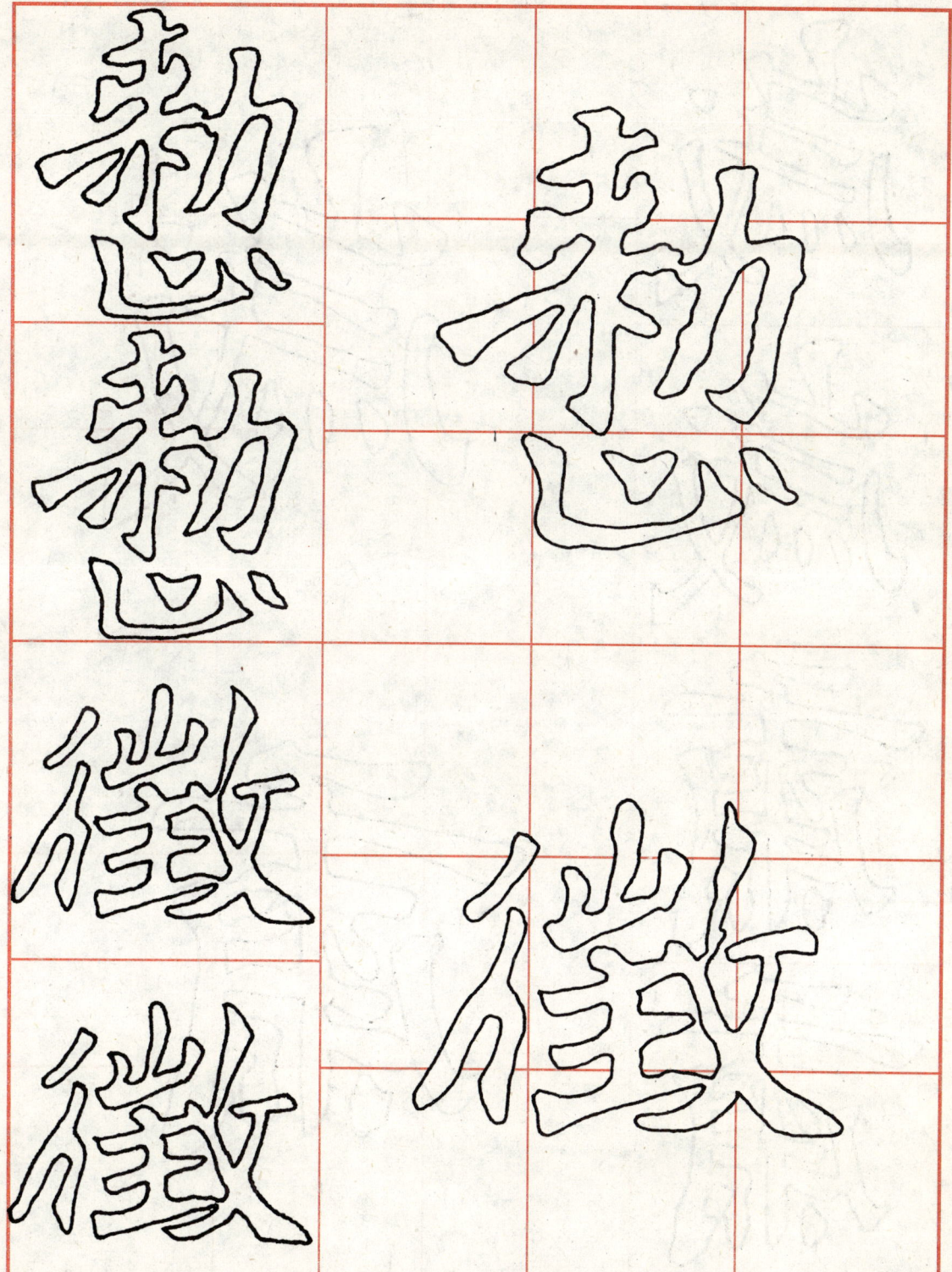

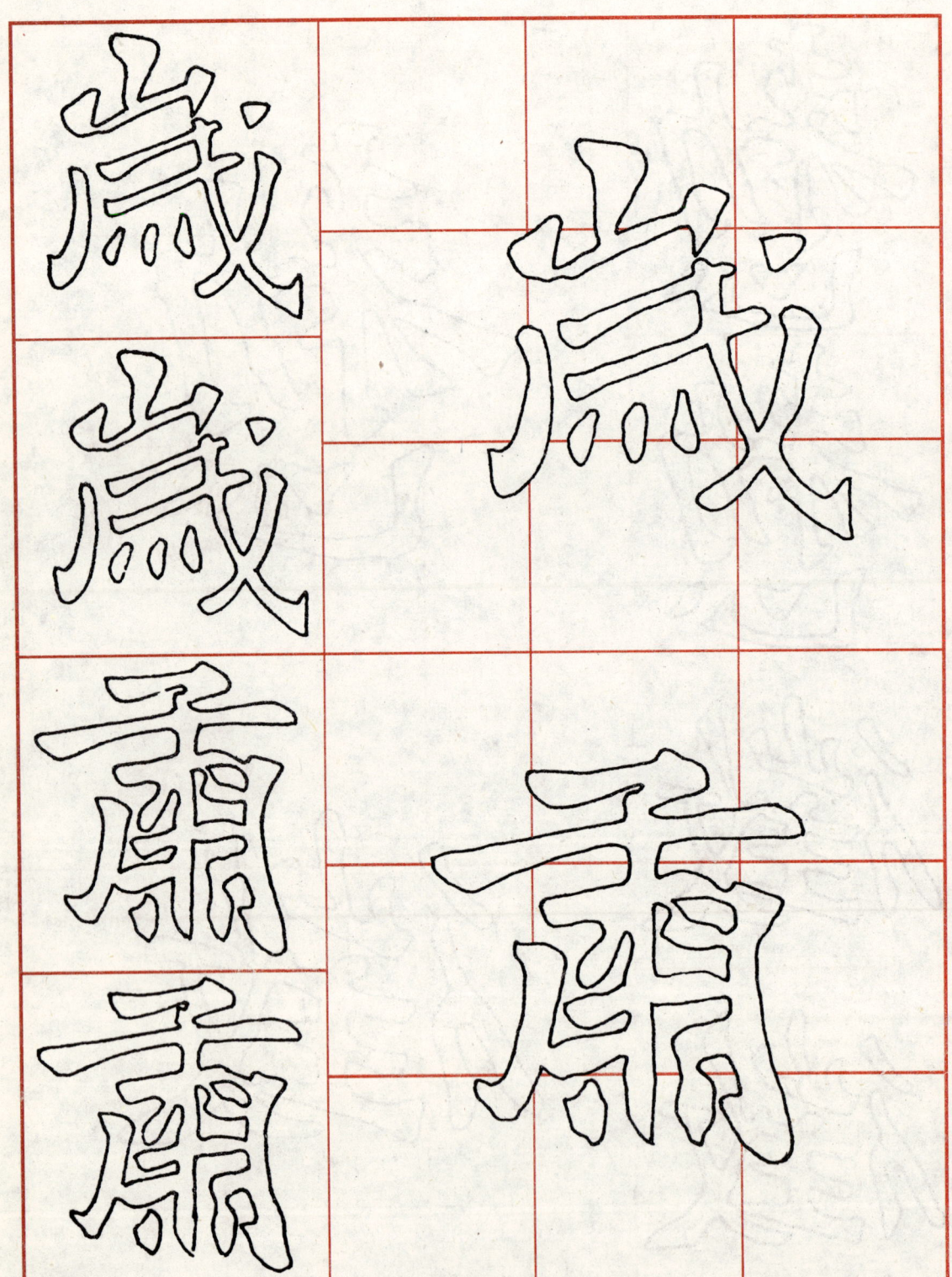

# 4. Two-Square Frame

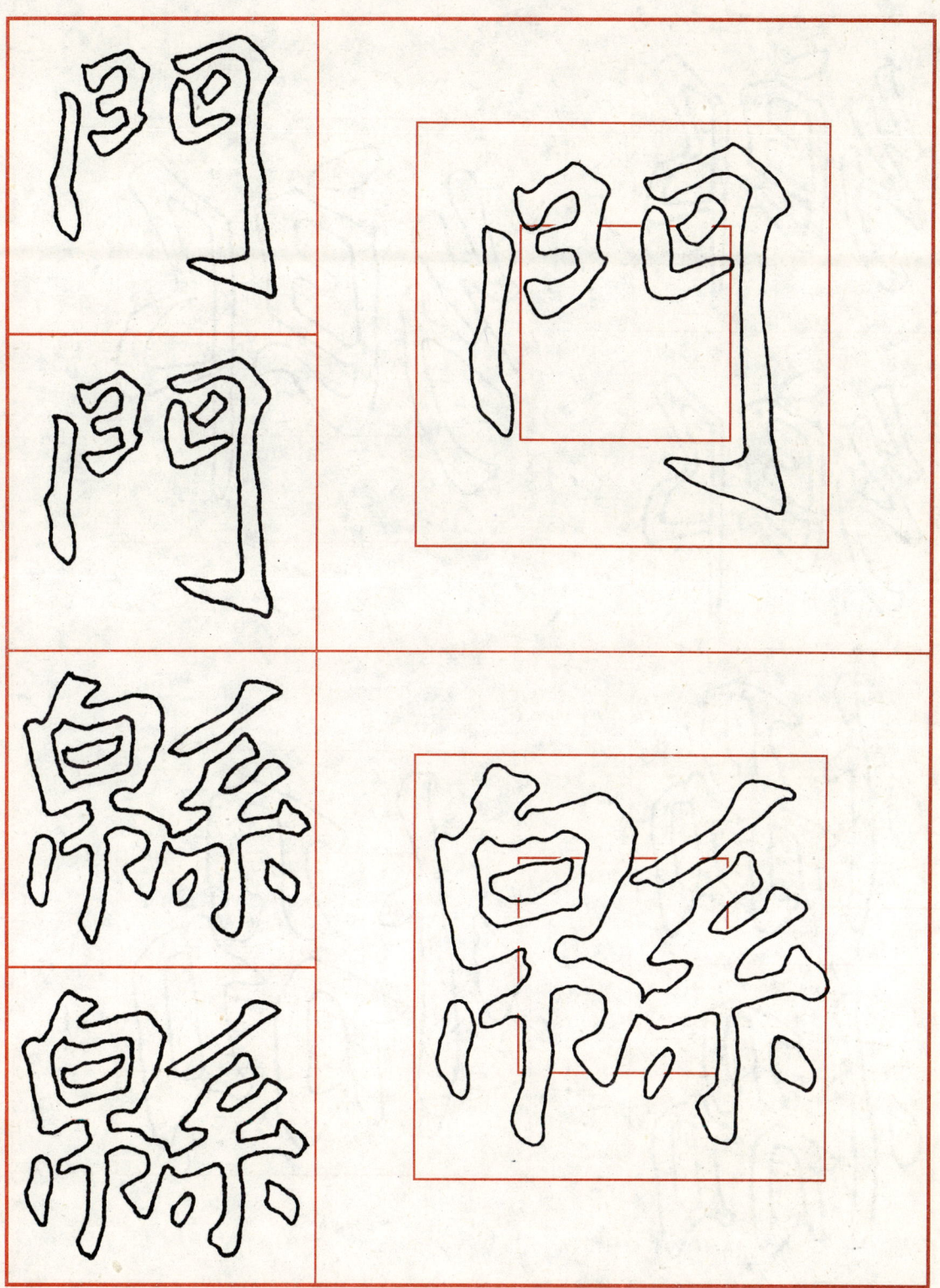

郷

郷

協

協

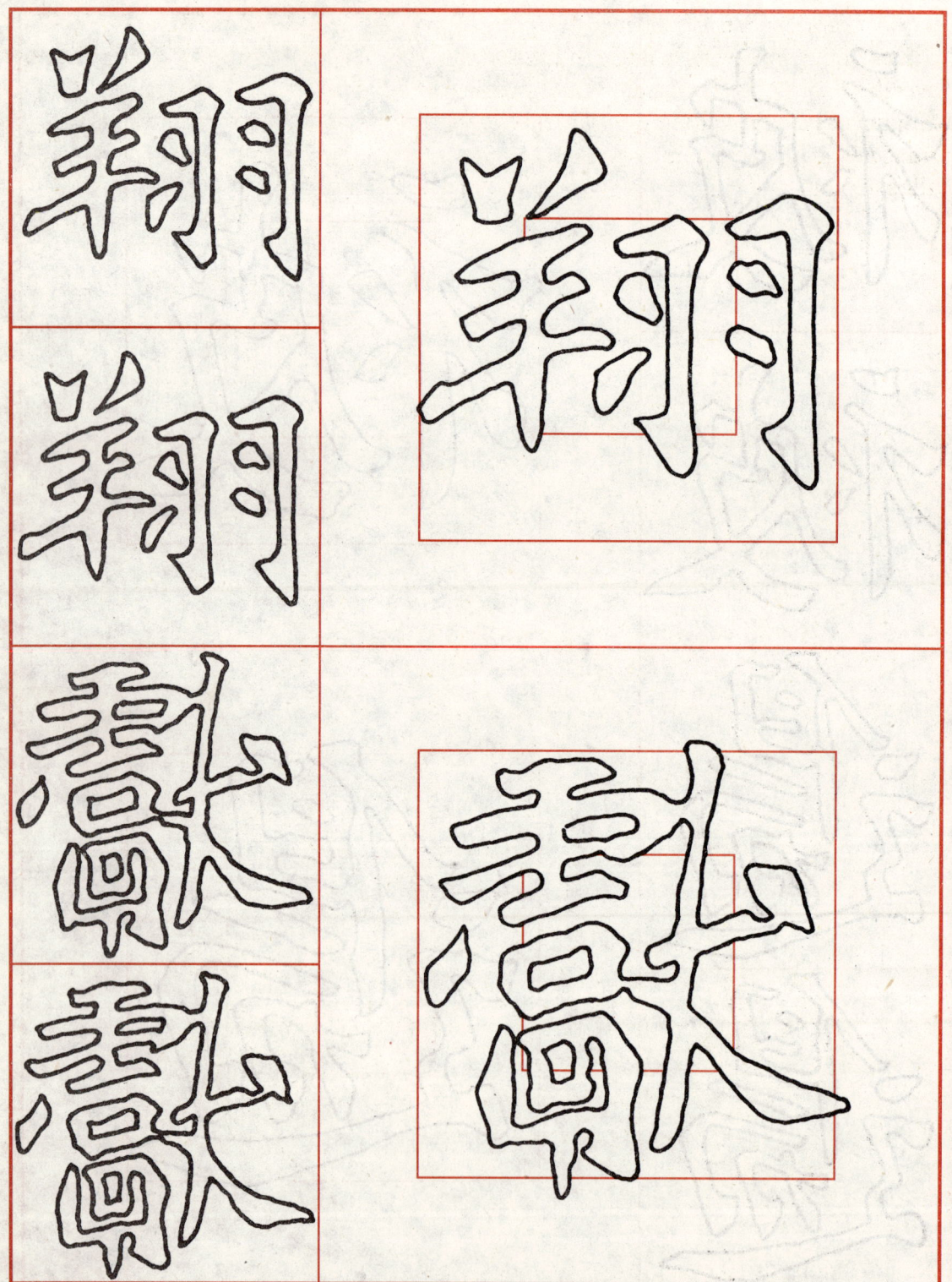

# Chapter VII   The Art of Composition

"A character consists of strokes; a line, characters; and an article, lines." A well written calligraphy work is made of many beautifully shaped characters, varying from several to over a thousand. While writing each stroke and each character, a calligrapher should take into consideration the beauty of the work as a whole. The arrangement of characters and lines is known as the art of composition, and was called as "outlay and format" by the people of ancient times.

# 1. Various Forms of Scrolls

There are various forms of scrolls of Chinese calligraphy, mainly including central scrolls, antithetical couplets, vertical-hung, square, horizontal and hand scrolls, albums of calligraphy, round or folding fans, horizontal or vertical inscribed boards and a set of scrolls (usually consisting of four, six, eight or twelve scrolls, each with separate or connected calligraphy works). A calligrapher adopts different forms of scrolls of Chinese calligraphy according to the actual needs and his/her appreciation. Different forms of scrolls are arranged in accordance with different arts of composition.

明月松間照

清泉石上流

摩詰維山居穐暝詩句

甲戌仲夏于渤北鳳賓齋主人

## 2. Text

The text is the main part of a work of calligraphy. The following three forms are commonly adopted: a. There are vertical lines and horizontal ranks, all characters arranged in good order. This form is frequently used by calligraphers creating works of regular, official and small seal scripts. b. There are vertical lines, but not horizontal ranks, making people feel that a well-arranged piece of calligraphy contains some changes. This form is mainly favorable to running script, and to other scripts as well. c. There are neither vertical lines nor horizontal ranks. Completely shaking off all pre-set forms, this form can make a calligrapher feel free to express his/her feelings and create whatever he/she wants. It is mainly suited to large seal and grass character scripts.

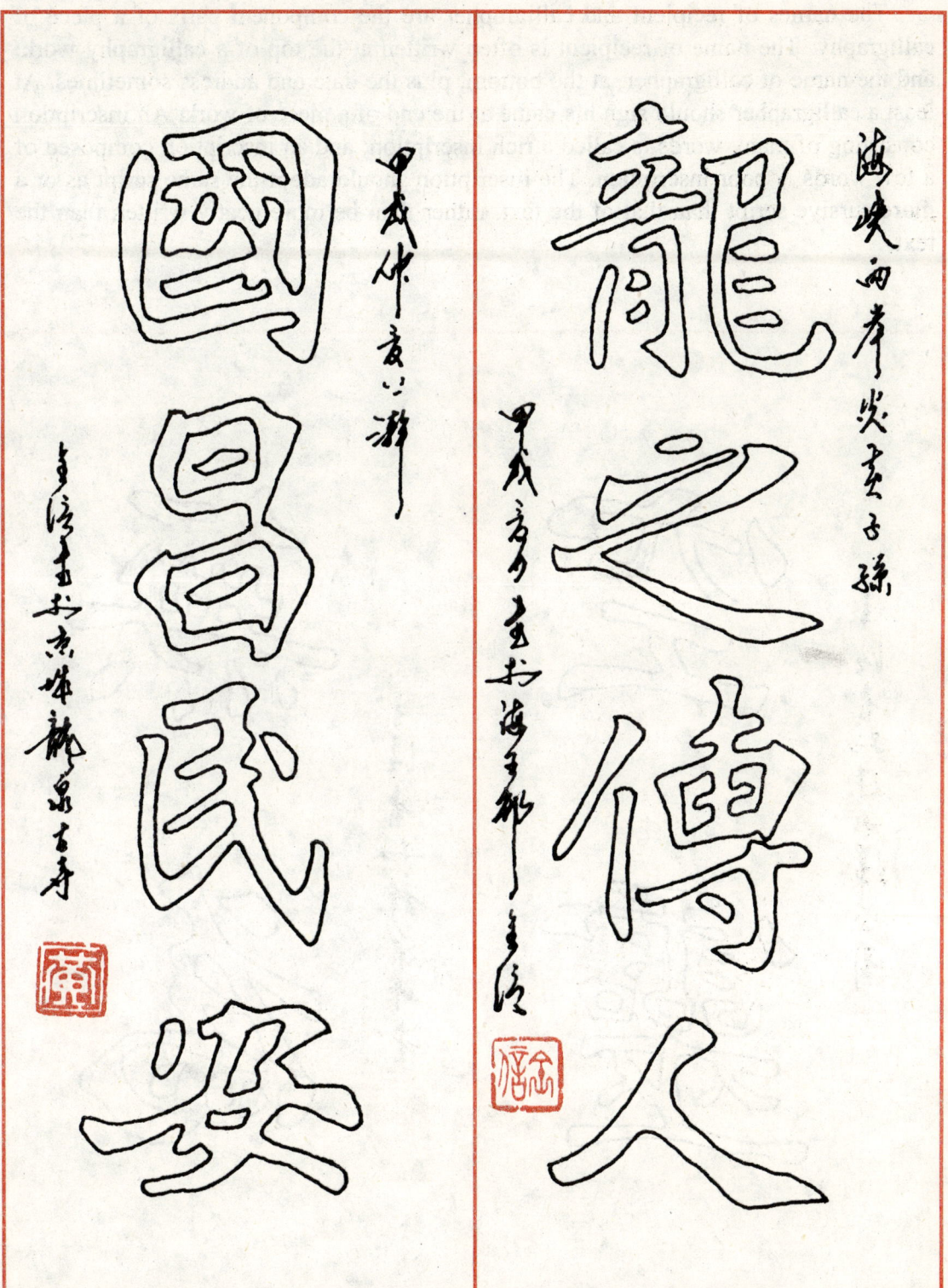

龍之傳人

滄峽兩岸炎黄子孫

甲戌秋月上書於滄海龍泉玉屏

國昌民安

甲戌仲夏之游

上清書於京華龍泉玉屏

# 3. Inscriptions

The names of recipient and calligrapher are the component parts of a piece of calligraphy. The name of recipient is often written at the top of a calligraphy work; and the name of calligrapher, at the bottom, plus the date and address sometimes. At least a calligrapher should sign his name at the end of a piece of work. An inscription consisting of many words is called a rich inscription; and an inscription composed of a few words, a poor inscription. The inscription should adopt the same script as or a more cursive script than that of the text, rather than be more neatly written than the text.

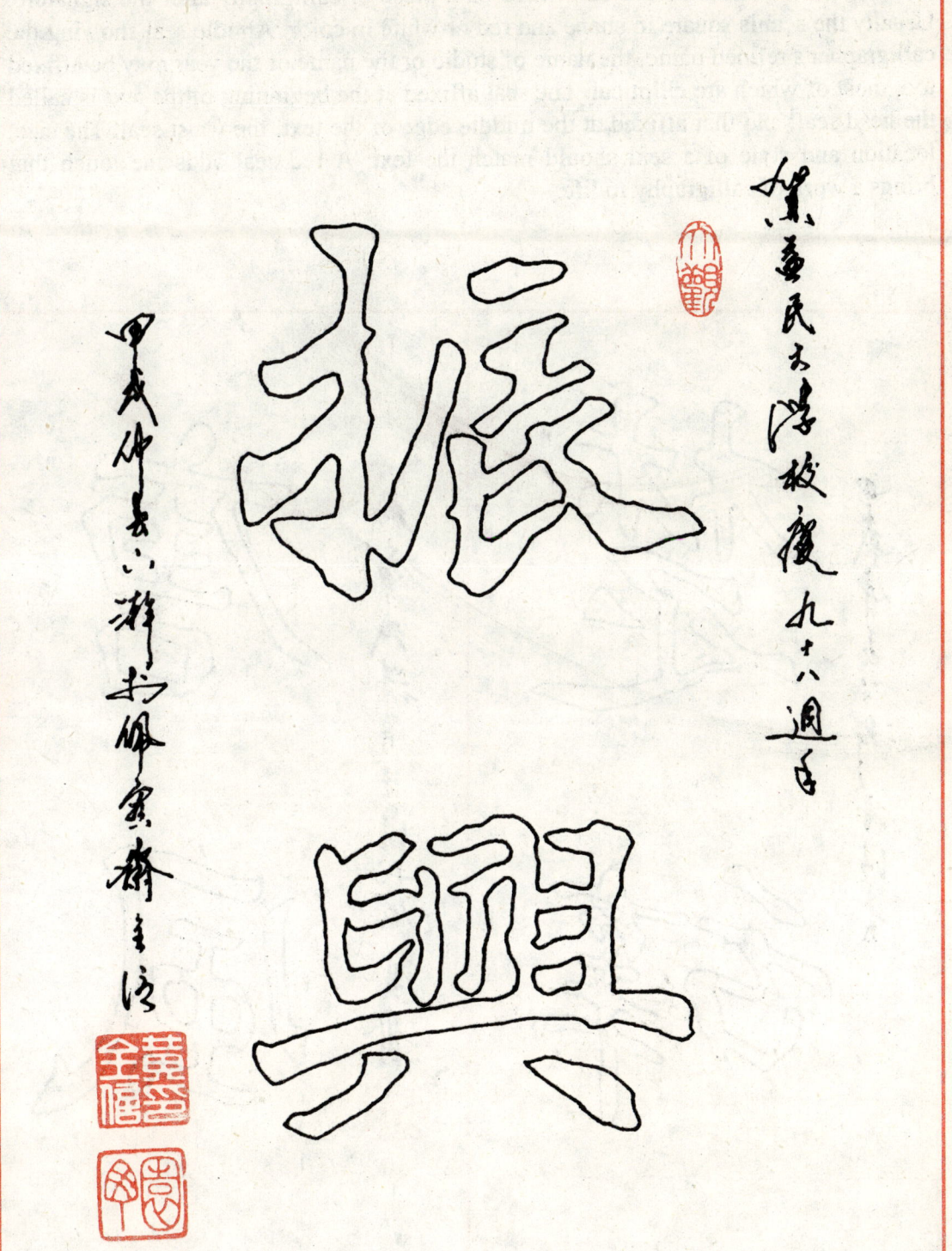

振興

慶華民六溽校覆九十六週年

甲戌仲春八澥書佩寶齋主沐

# 4. Seals

In general, a seal should be affixed on a piece of calligraphy after the signature. Usually the seal is square in shape and red or white in color. An idle seal showing the calligrapher's refined name, the name of studio or the name of the year may be affixed too, most of which are elliptical. The seal affixed at the beginning of the text is called the head seal; and that affixed at the middle edge of the text, the waist seal. The size, location and style of a seal should match the text. A red seal adds the touch that brings a work of calligraphy to life.

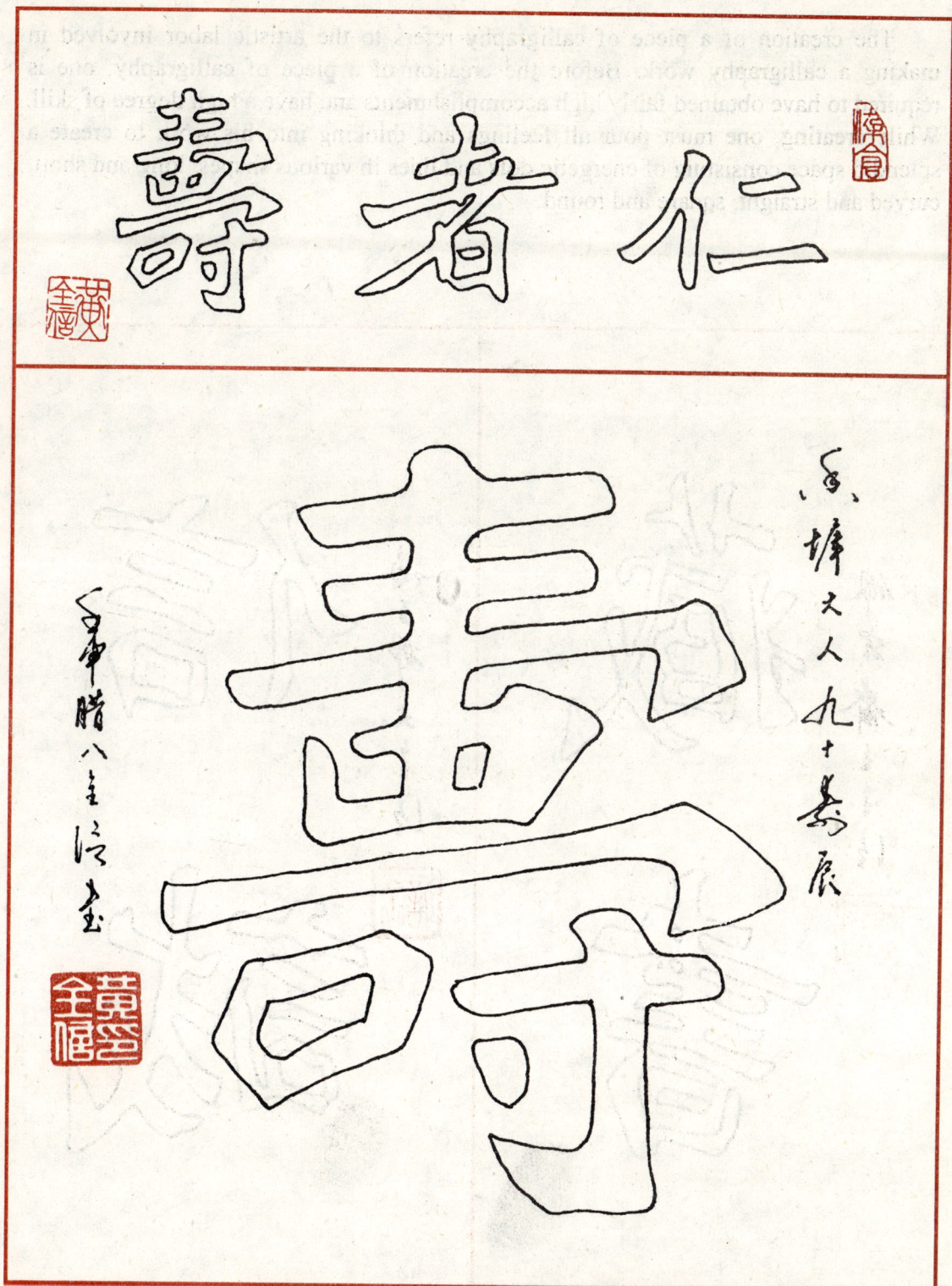

# Chapter VIII    Creation

The creation of a piece of calligraphy refers to the artistic labor involved in making a calligraphy work. Before the creation of a piece of calligraphy, one is required to have obtained fairly high accomplishments and have a high degree of skill. While creating, one must pour all feelings and thinking into his work to create a splendid space consisting of energetic dots and lines in various shapes, long and short, curved and straight, square and round.

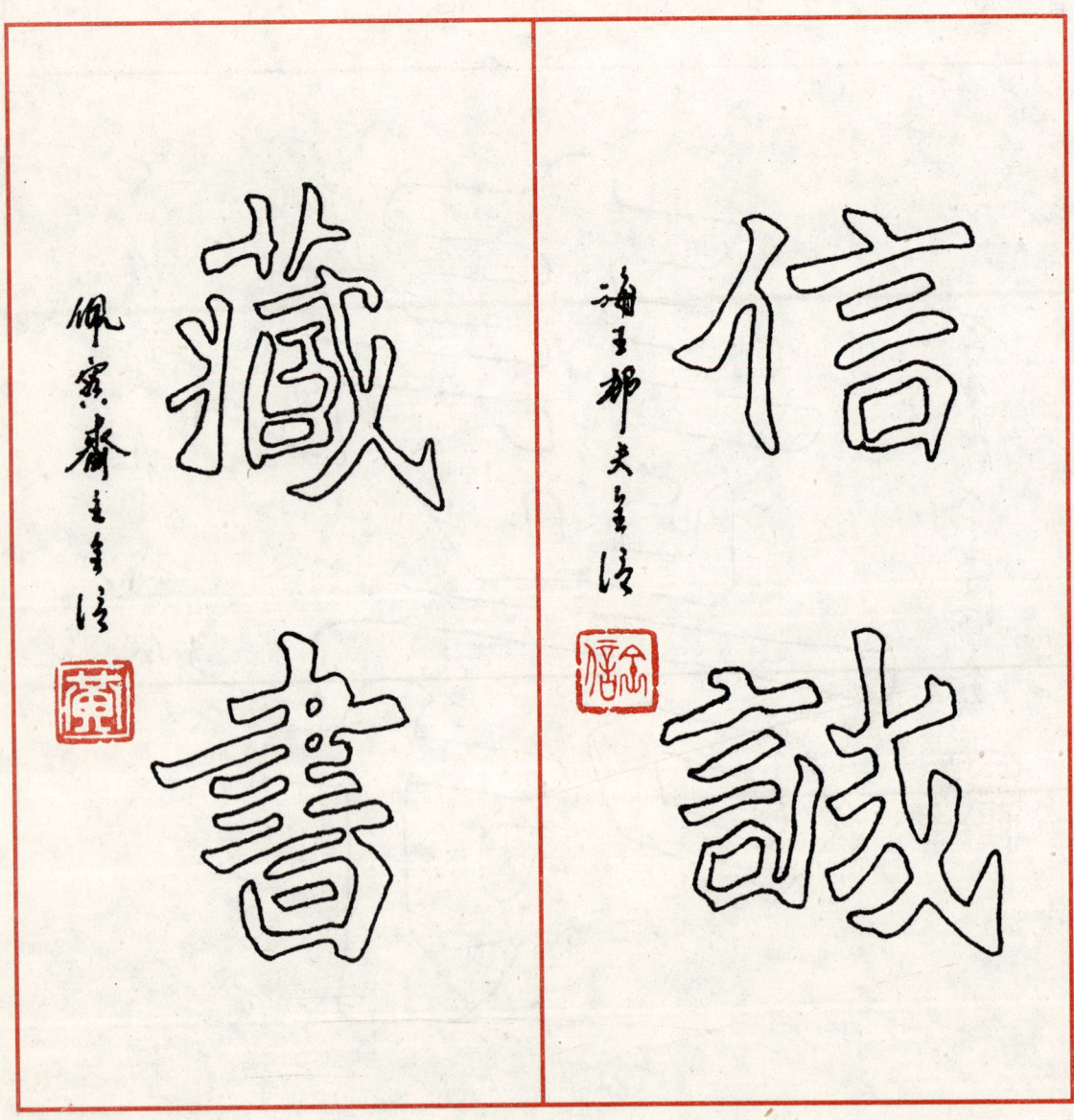

## 1. Making a Plan Before Writing

Before one starts writing, one should make a well-thought plan concerning the text, inscription, seal, etc. One should decide how to write characters according to the size of a piece of paper, concentrate one's mind on the brush, spread out the paper prudently and start writing the first stroke resolutely. The more profound significance of making a plan is to express the realm that the calligrapher seeks through a concrete calligraphy work. This is hard because it is so abstract. The Chinese calligraphers of the past ages paid great attention to making a plan, believing that the plan plays a leading role in creation.

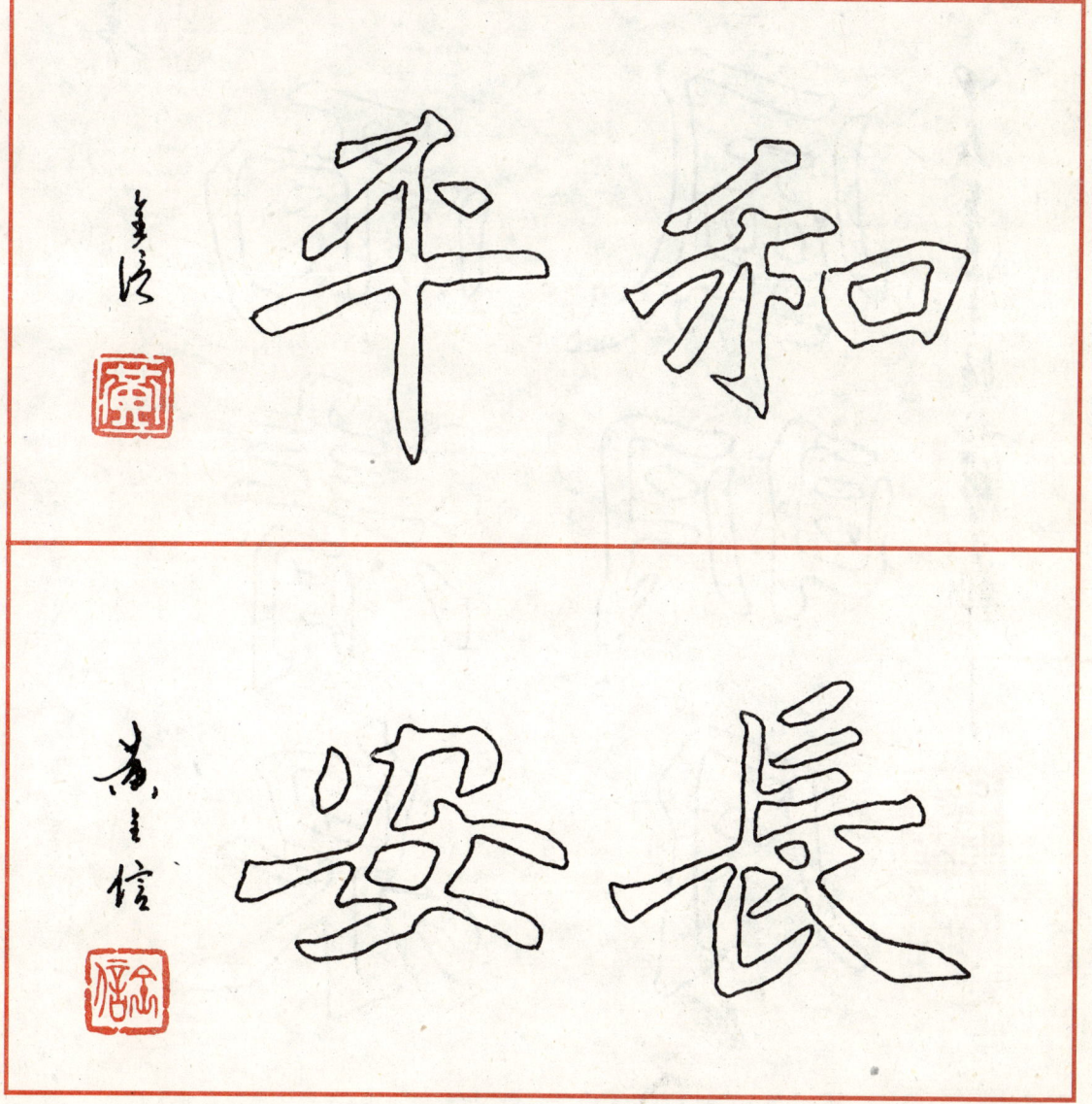

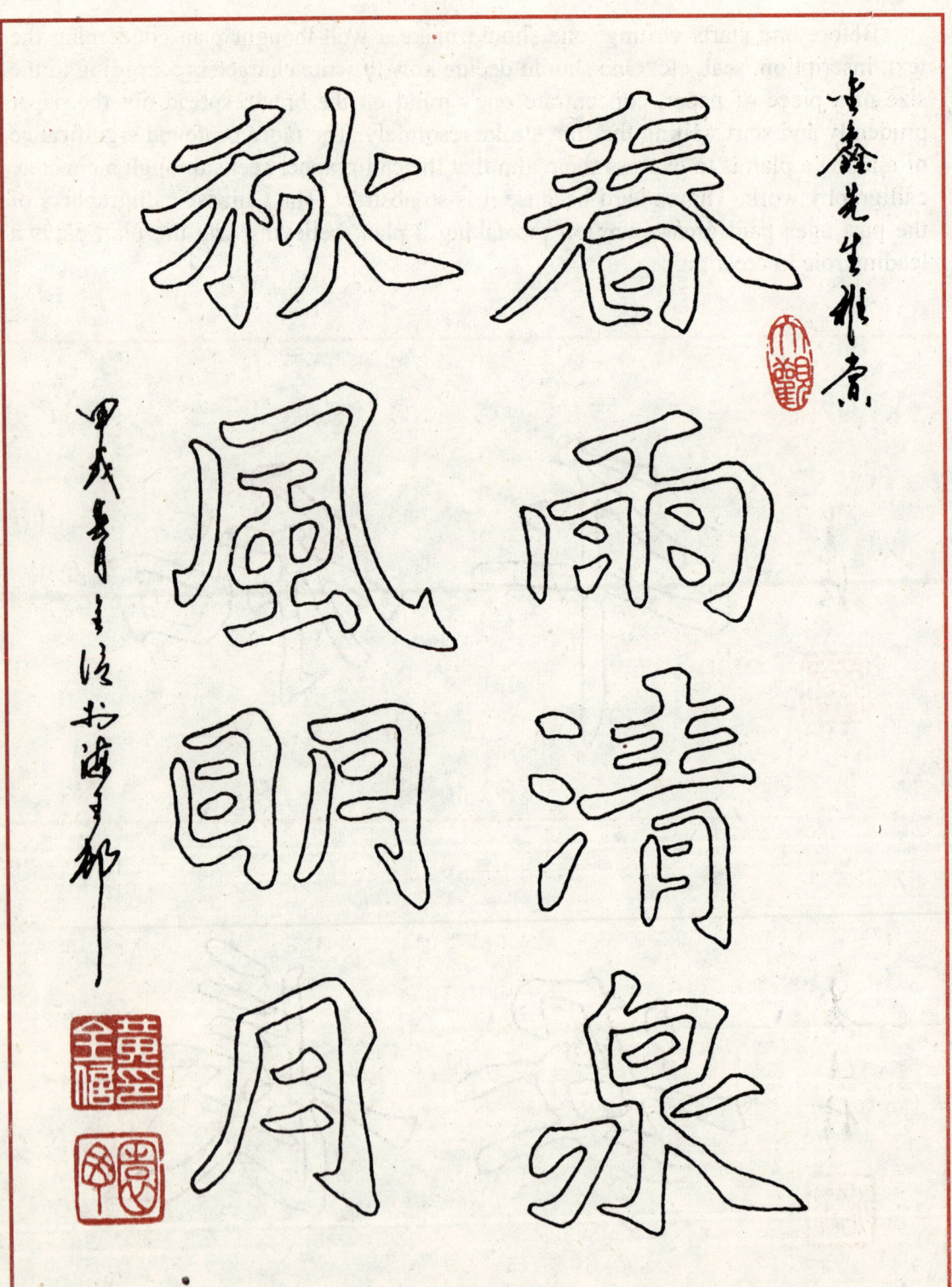

春雨清泉
秋風明月

云鑫先生雅正

甲戌春月全澄於滬上

## 2. The First Character Leads the Whole Text

"The first stroke sets the standards for a character, and the first character leads all characters of an article." This is a brilliant exposition in the *Calligraphy Manual* by Sun Guoting, a famous calligrapher of the Tang Dynasty, stressing the importance of the first stroke in the first character and the first character in a text.

The first character takes the lead of a calligraphy work. Writing the first character well is just like a horse running ahead, followed by ten thousand galloping horses.

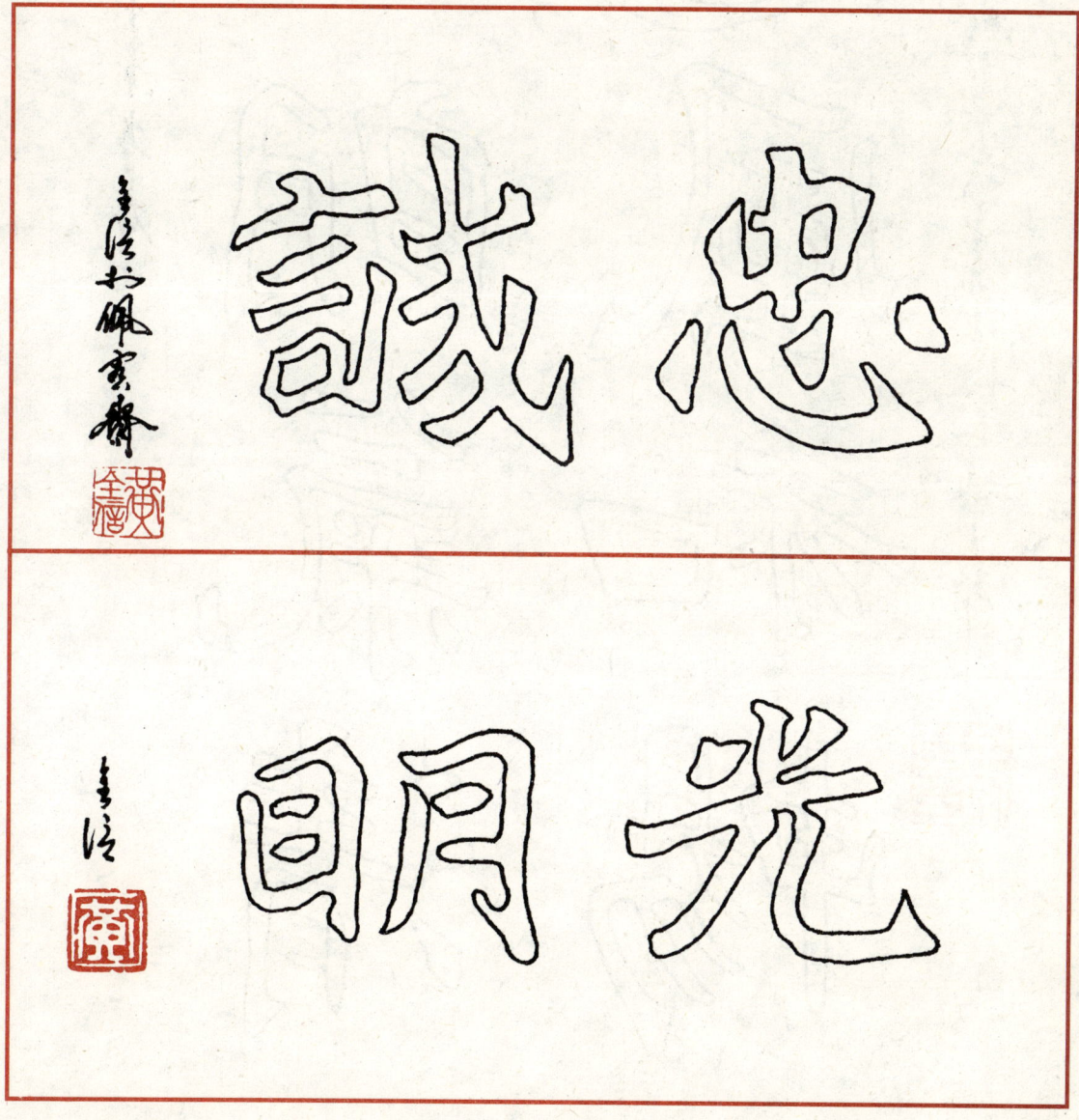

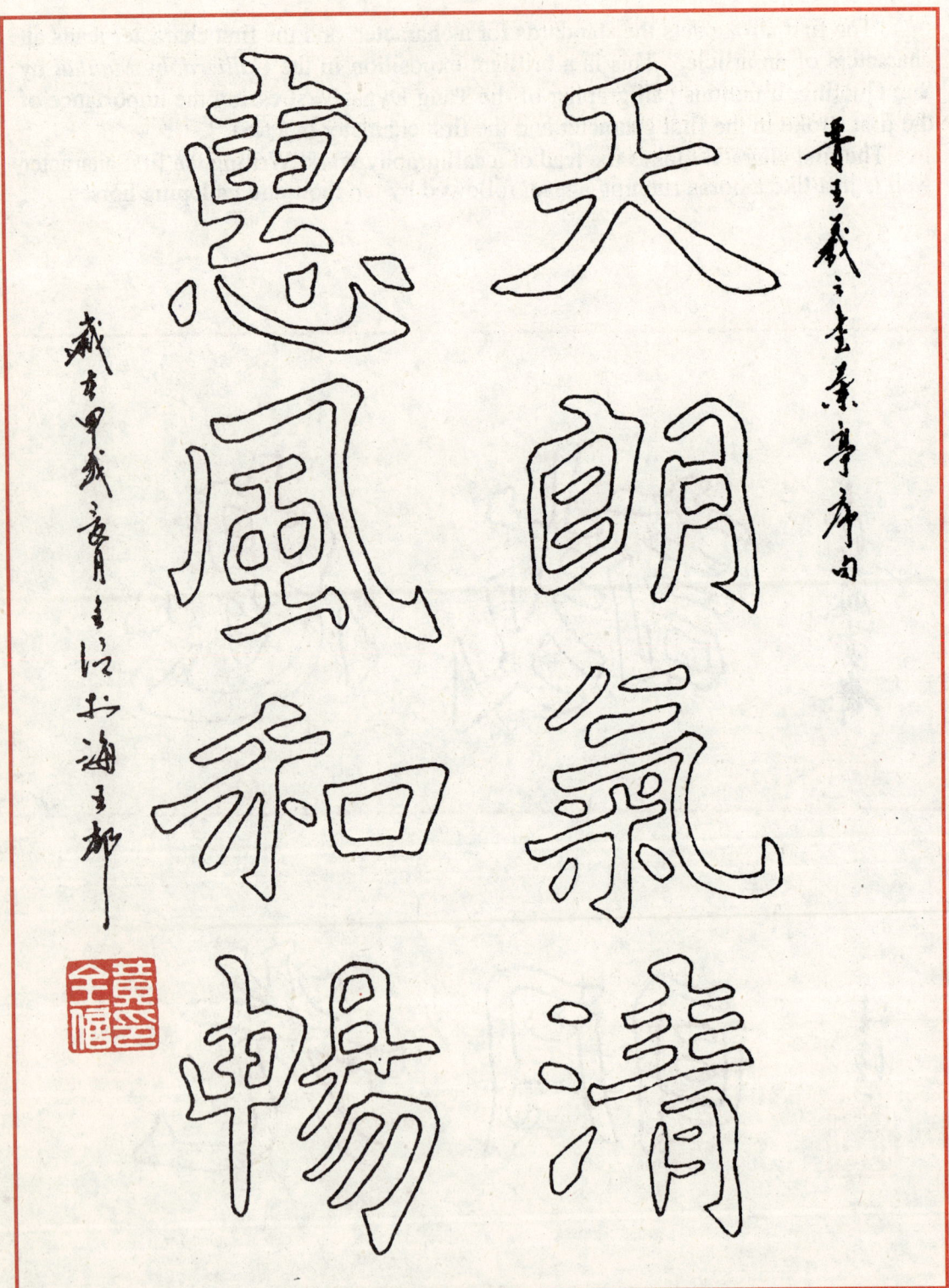

天朗氣清
惠風和暢

晉王羲之蘭亭序句

歲在甲戌青月書於北海王都

## 3. A Coherent Whole

Chinese calligraphy is particular about coherence. Finishing a calligraphy work (including the text, inscription, signature, etc.) at one go aims at capturing a unified internal spirit of a work. Coherence should exist throughout a piece of calligraphy, between characters and lines, which echo each other and are integrated into one, showing united spirit and charm as a whole.

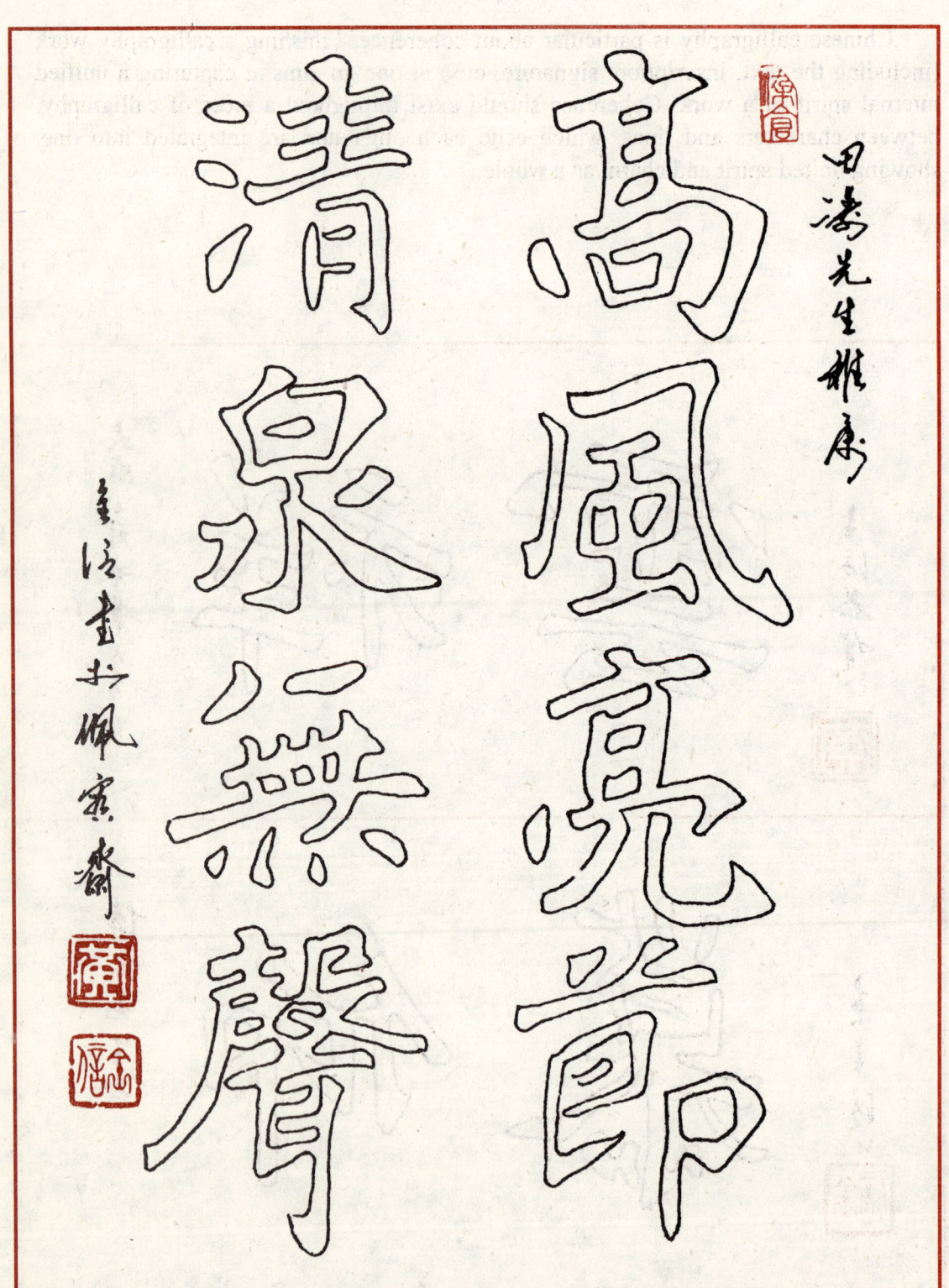

高風亮節

清泉無聲

田濤先生雅屬

壬冱畫於佩紫水齋

## 4. A Poetic Conception

"A calligrapher expresses his feelings through his works." Before creation, a calligrapher should fully understand the meaning of a poem as well as its literacy grace, and should know well the author's internal feelings. Only if one enters a poetic conception, can one fully express one's own feelings and correctly convey the poet's sentiments. In addition, a calligrapher should pay attention to the unification of the script, style, and contents.

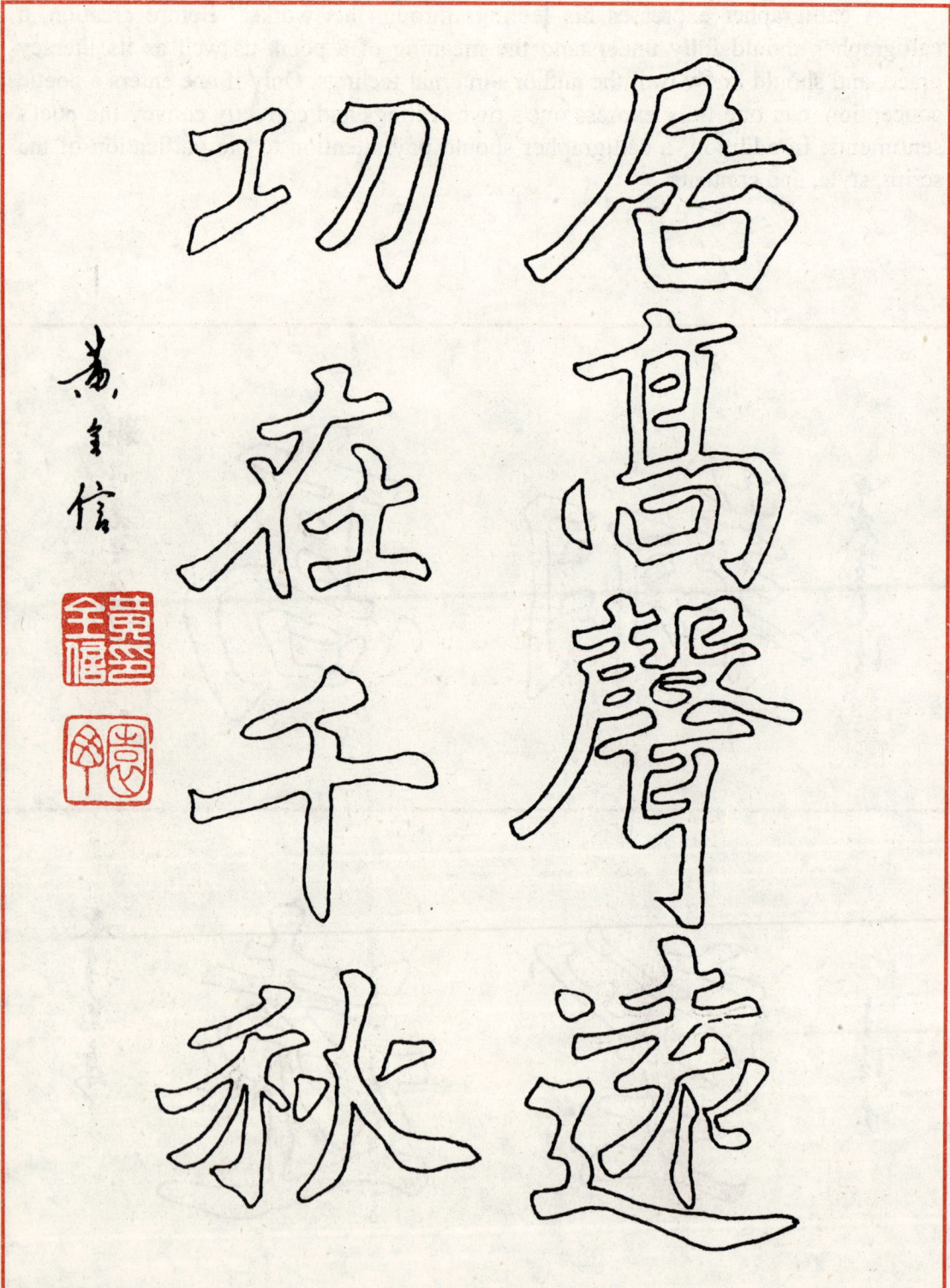

居高聲遠

功在千秋

蘇童信

# Chapter IX    Appreciation

To improve the art of calligraphy, one should first copy one calligraphy model until one has a good command it, and then copy various calligraphy models by different famous calligraphers; and then appreciate various calligraphy works of the past ages to constantly absorb nutrition and improve the appreciation level.

In addition, one is required to read a large number of books, make many trips, read numerous tablets and copy models of various schools.

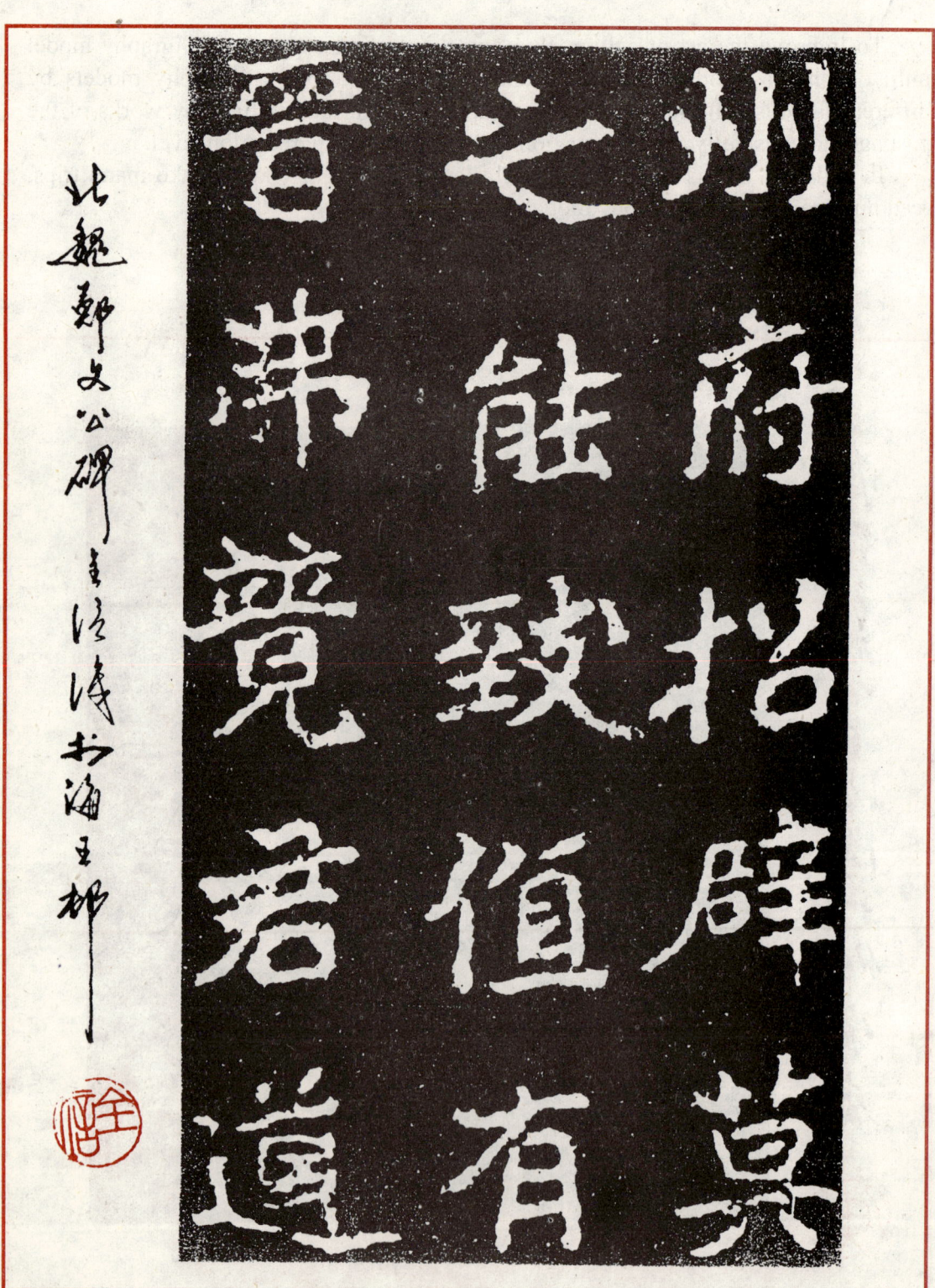

州府招辟莫

之能致

晋弟竟

君道

北魏郑文公碑 王临海王柳书

魚吏部郎詮敘彝倫九
流斯順太和廿二年春
宣武皇帝創光崇正妙
蘭宮衛復以君為東朝
步兵景明初丁母憂還

功廉作輔國將軍直開國子仇池揚大眼始於弱年挺超群於万於一掌震英勇則於三紛掃雲勵於天

责任编辑　单　瑛

封面设计　朱　丹　黄全信


**图书在版编目（CIP）数据**

魏碑自学教程／黄全信编著．－北京：华语教学出版社，1997.3

（中国书法自学丛书）ISBN 7-80052-457-4

Ⅰ．魏…　Ⅱ．黄…　Ⅲ．汉字－楷书－自学参考资料　Ⅳ.J292.11

中国版本图书馆 CIP 数据核字（97）第 00819 号


中国书法自学丛书—魏碑自学教程

黄全信　编著

*

©华语教学出版社

华语教学出版社出版

（中国北京百万庄路 24 号）

邮政编码 100037

春雷印刷厂印刷

中国国际图书贸易总公司发行

（中国北京车公庄西路 35 号）

北京邮政信箱第 399 号　邮政编码 100044

1998 年（16 开）第一版

（汉英）

ISBN 7-80052-457-4／H · 549（外）

03500

9 - CE - 3195P